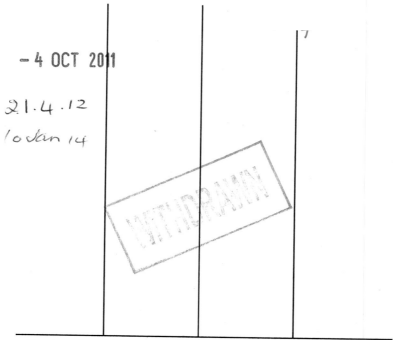

THE HIDDEN THREAT

*Dedicated to the brave men who kept the sea lanes open,
and saved the Allied cause between 1914 and 1919.*

THE HIDDEN THREAT

THE STORY OF MINES AND MINESWEEPING BY THE ROYAL NAVY IN WORLD WAR I

BY

JIM CROSSLEY

Pen & Sword
MARITIME

First published in Great Britain in 2011 by
Pen & Sword Maritime
an imprint of
Pen & Sword Books Ltd
47 Church Street
Barnsley
South Yorkshire
S70 2AS

Copyright © Jim Crossley 2011

ISBN 978-1-84884-272-4

A CIP catalogue record for this book is available from the British Library.

Typeset in 11.5pt Ehrhardt by
Mac Style, Beverley, E. Yorkshire

Printed and bound in the UK by the MPG Books Group

Pen & Sword Books Ltd incorporates the Imprints of Pen & Sword Aviation, Pen & Sword Maritime, Pen & Sword Military, Wharncliffe Local History, Pen and Sword Select, Pen and Sword Military Classics, Leo Cooper, Remember When, Seaforth Publishing and Frontline Publishing.

For a complete list of Pen & Sword titles please contact
PEN & SWORD BOOKS LIMITED
47 Church Street, Barnsley, South Yorkshire, S70 2AS, England
E-mail: enquiries@pen-and-sword.co.uk
Website: www.pen-and-sword.co.uk

Contents

List of Figures vii

'The Minesweepers' by Rudyard Kipling viii

Introduction 1

1 Origins 9

2 Mines and the Royal Navy 21

3 German Minelaying and the British Response 45

4 The Gallipoli Campaign 97

5 The British Mine-laying Offensive 111

6 Clearing Up 149

7 Conclusion 159

Index 163

List of Figures

1. A Leon mine   13
2. The Hertz horn   18
3. The plummet system   24
4. German 'egg' mine   25
5. The British Naval Spherical Mine   26
6. Conventionl minesweeping gear   28
7. A German submarine-laid mine   66
8. German UCII Class U-boat   67
9. Comparison between German UCII and UEII Class U-boats   67
10. The defensive paravane   73
11. The high speed sweep   82
12. The Oropesa sweep   83
13. The electro-contact mined net   121
14. The British H.II mine   123
15. Antenna Mine   142
16. Magnetic Ground Mine   147

Charts

1. The East Coast Swept Channel and other North Sea and English Channel swept channels   55
2. British, German and American mines laid during World War One   62
3. Dardanelles showing minefields and defences   99
4. The Folkstone – Griz Nez Barrage in 1918   133

The Minesweepers
By Rudyard Kipling

Dawn off the Foreland-the young flood making
Jumbled and short and steep – black in the hollows
   and bright where it's breaking
Awkward water to sweep.
'Mines reported in the fairway. Warn all shipping and
   detain
Sent up *Unity, Claribel, Assyrian, Stormcock* and *Golden
   Gain.'*

Noon off the Foreland-the first ebb making
Lumpy and strong in the bight.
Boom after boom, and the golf hut shaking
And the jackdaws wild with fright.
'Mines located in the fairway,
Boats now working up the chain.
Sweepers *Unity, Claribel, Assyrian, Stormcock* and *Golden
   Gain.'*

Dusk off the Foreland-the last light going
And the traffic crowding through
And five damned trawlers with their syreens blowing
Heading the whole review!
'Sweep completed in the fairway.
No more mines remain.
Send back *Unity, Claribel, Assyrian, Stormcock* and *Golden
   Gain.'*

Introduction

On 26 October 1914 the Second Battle Squadron of the Royal Navy (2BS) put to sea for exercises, they were to fire their main armament at targets towed by two tugs, *Plover* and *Flying Condor*, and they were escorted by the light cruiser *Liverpool*. 2BS consisted of five ships, its strength would normally have been eight but three of them were in dock for various reasons. They were all 'super dreadnought' battleships with names redolent of the great days of the Royal Navy – *King George V*, *Audacious*, *Centurion*, *Monarch* and *Thunderer*. The nation expected from them a performance to equal that of the heroic age of the British maritime power in the days of Nelson, St Vincent, Hawke and a host of other magnificent figures from previous centuries. These super dreadnoughts were all products of the 1909 and 1910 building programmes of the Royal Navy. They represented the epitome of contemporary naval technology. They displaced 22,500 to 23,000 tons and were capable of a top speed of about 21 knots. They had the advantage of their German peers in speed and weight of broadside (13.5-inch guns as against 12-inch), but were slightly less heavily armoured. The commander of this formidable squadron was Vice Admiral Sir George Warrender Bt KCB. Warrender was in every respect typical of the admirals of the Royal Navy of the time. He was brave as a lion, aristocratic, popular with his subordinates and able to use his considerable personal charm to inspire loyalty and devotion among the officers and seamen under his command. Unfortunately, his training and upbringing made him incapable of comprehending the threats or the realities of warfare in the twentieth century. One of his contemporaries, Commodore 'Barge' Goodenough, remarked admiringly on his possession of 'An imperturbability that no circumstances could ruffle' – others attributed his calm to the fact that he seldom understood the magnitude of the problem.

The terrible dangers faced by the Grand Fleet – as the mighty force under command of Admiral Sir John Jellicoe was known – had already been brought home pretty comprehensively to its Commander-in-Chief. The fleet war anchorage at Scapa Flow had been plagued by the real or imaginary appearance of German submarines since the outbreak of the war. Further south, three old cruisers had been torpedoed in quick succession by a U-boat on 22 September with the loss of 1,400 lives. Concluding that his ships were unsafe at Scapa, Jellicoe had moved the fleet anchorage, first to Loch Ewe on the west coast of Scotland, then even further away to Loch-na-Keal on the Isle of Mull, which had a narrow and easily protected entrance, and to Loch Swilly in the north of Ireland, also easily defended. It was incomprehensible to many of his countrymen, who confidently expected an early victory at sea on the scale of Trafalgar, that the greatest battle fleet in the world could be driven to take shelter so far away from its base by a handful of primitive submarines. But Jellicoe realized that he was facing an entirely new type of naval warfare. In previous ages big warships were immune to attack by smaller ones. A nineteenth century sloop, for example, had no chance whatever of sinking a battleship, but the advent of high-explosive torpedoes and mines had turned the established norms on their head. A torpedo fired by a 130-ton submarine, or a speeding torpedo boat, a mine laid by a stealthy trawler or a disguised railway ferry: in 1914 these represented deadly threats to the mightiest super dreadnought. Seeing the threat very clearly, Jellicoe wrote a paper to cover himself in case he was considered lacking in fighting spirit by his superiors. He feared that his enemy might try to feign flight so as to lure his big ships onto a trap set by submarines or by a minefield. He knew that all German warships had facilities for dropping mines over the stern when they were being chased and regarded this as a grave danger. He wrote to the Admiralty:

> If for instance the enemy battle fleet were to turn away from our advancing fleet I would assume it was to lead us over mines or submarines and refuse to be drawn. I desire particularly to draw the attention of their Lordships to this point since it may be deemed a refusal of battle and might possibly result in failure to bring the enemy to action as soon as it is expected. Such a result would be absolutely repugnant to the feelings of all British naval officers and men, but with new untried methods of warfare, new tactics must be devised... (These) if not understood properly, may bring odium on me, but so long as I have the confidence of their Lordships, I intend to pursue the proper course to defeat and annihilate the enemy's battle fleet without regard for uninstructed opinion or criticism. The situation is a difficult one: it is quite possible that half

of our battle fleet might be disabled by underwater attack before the great guns opened fire at all...

In writing this Jellicoe showed himself to be a thinking admiral who clearly understood the strategic imperative of keeping the battle fleet in being, and superior to its enemy. In the event, he probably over stated the danger from submarines; the boats available in 1914 were not destined to have much success against fast moving warships, but his fear of mines was certainly justified.

In its new bases, however, the fleet considered itself safe and the normal training regime was resumed. The sortie by 2BS was part of this training and as the ships were off the north coast of Donegal, about nineteen miles from Tory Island, they believed they were outside effective U-boat range. The ships seem to have reverted to almost peacetime procedures. They were not closed up for action and watertight doors, which would have divided the hulls into secure watertight compartments, were left open. *Audacious* was the third ship in the column. Completed a year earlier, she was considered a 'crack ship' and her Captain, Cecil Dampier, was keen to show off her gunnery skills. At 08.45 hours Warrender ordered his column to turn four points to starboard. *Audacious* was a little out of station and answered her helm slowly. Just as she began to swing onto her new course, a massive explosion detonated on the port side of the hull, aft of the main mast, flooding the port engine room and sending clouds of steam belching from the after funnel and out through any open hatches. Luckily, the steam vented clear of the men in the engine room and no one was hurt. Men stuck bravely to their posts until ordered on deck. The ship listed sharply to port as the watertight doors were belatedly closed. Following standing instructions, the rest of 2BS steamed on regardless. It was suspected that the explosion must have been caused by a torpedo, and, if so, it was vital to keep moving and get clear of the area as soon as possible. One light cruiser, *Liverpool*, and two destroyers were ordered to stand by the stricken battleship, but to keep moving so as to make a difficult target for the suspected submarine.

But it was not a submarine that had caused the damage. The fast liner *Berlin* (17,000 tons) had been hurriedly fitted out as an armed merchant cruiser, with 6-inch guns and a complement of 200 deadly mines. Both sides made extensive use of armed merchant ships like *Berlin* during the war, often in high risk operations. They frequently had much longer ranges than warships and were relatively easy to disguise as neutrals; also, navies probably considered them and their crews more expendable than warships. *Berlin* had been ordered to mine the mouth of the River Clyde in the hope of laying a trap for some of the transports carrying Canadian troops to Britain. These were expected to arrive late in October (actually, unknown to the Germans, they had been diverted to the south coast while en route). Captain Pfundheller of *Berlin* had set sail in mid-October. His voyage was covered for the most part by a welcome blanket of fog, so he was able to avoid detection by British patrols and arrived somewhere near his destination on the 24th. At that time ships had no way of fixing their position precisely in thick weather, and mines have to be laid accurately and in the correct depth of water or they are useless. After vainly trying to find out exactly where he was, Pfundheller decided that that he could hang about so close to the Scottish coast no longer and turned westward, so as to drop his deadly cargo in the shipping lanes just north east of Tory Island, where they might catch merchant shipping bound for Britain. Having accomplished his mission, he turned *Berlin* northward to get clear of the dangerous waters so near the British fleet, and to seek unprotected British merchantmen trading with Russia or Norway. Off northern Norway, *Berlin* encountered a heavy gale that damaged the ship and forced her to enter Trondheim for repair. Here she was identified and, together with her crew, interned for the rest of the war.

Berlin had not sailed in vain. On the night of 25 October the steamer *Manchester Commerce* struck one of her mines and sank. A few hours later the four-masted sailing ship *Caldaff* suffered the same fate. No reports of these sinkings were sent to Jellicoe, so no particular warnings of mines were circulated to the Grand Fleet. The absence of such warning, however, does not excuse Warrender's carelessness in putting to sea without ordering the ships in his squadron to close their watertight doors.

Audacious still had her starboard engines working and was able to make nine knots under her own power, so it was decided to try to struggle to Loch Swilly to beach her. However, the water was rising fast and she was clearly going to need help. Small vessels were sent out to her from the fleet anchorage and the old battleship *Exmouth* was ordered to raise steam in case a tow was needed. (Jellicoe, still thinking that a submarine was responsible, didn't want to risk a dreadnought. *Exmouth* was expendable.) At 10.50 hours, about two hours after the original explosion, the remaining engines stopped and Dampier began to send most of the crew away in boats to the attendant small ships. Some 250 volunteers stayed on board to try to save the battleship. Hopes rose when the mighty 45,000-ton White

Star liner *Olympic* (sister ship to *Titanic*) arrived on the scene after an Atlantic crossing. Her appropriately named Captain Haddock signalled that he would do what he could to help. Showing commendable seamanship in deteriorating weather conditions, the collier *Thornhill* and the destroyer *Fury* passed lines between the two big ships and the tow commenced. The sea, however, was rising, and as she filled with water *Audacious* became impossible to tow, hawsers were constantly breaking as she wallowed deeper and deeper in the water. At 19.45 hours, all personnel were evacuated from the stricken dreadnought. At 21.00 hours she suddenly exploded and sank. What caused the explosion was never determined, but it led to the only casualty of the episode. A large splinter struck and killed a petty officer on *Liverpool*, which was still standing by. Amazingly, *Audacious* had been fatally damaged by a fairly small mine, containing only 160 lb of guncotton, intended to sink merchant ships. Many much smaller ships survived mines containing over 500 lb of explosive, and German dreadnoughts on many occasions managed to carry on operating after striking quite large Allied mines. This indicates how poorly the British battleships were designed as far as underwater protection is concerned.

Earlier in the afternoon, Jellicoe had been belatedly informed of the loss of *Manchester Commerce* and *Caldaff*, and was able to conclude that a mine, not a torpedo, was responsible for the disasters. He took immediate steps to divert all traffic away from Tory Island and ordered minesweepers to clear a passage. Great efforts were made to cover up the news of the disaster, but as there were American passengers on *Olympic* who had photographed the ship sinking, these were of little effect. Nevertheless, no official announcement was made until after the war. Secrecy was important as at that stage of the war the Grand Fleet only just outnumbered its opponents, having seventeen effective dreadnought battleships against Germany's fifteen, and both sides had just five battle cruisers. If ever Germany had a chance against the Grand Fleet, it was in October 1914.

After the loss of *Audacious*, no naval operation could ignore the danger of mines. The results speak for themselves. During the whole of the 1914–1918 war, *Audacious* was the only dreadnought battleship lost for any reason either by Britain or by Germany. (Austria lost two, one to a limpet mine and one to a torpedo boat.) Not one was lost to gunfire. Mines caused far more losses to the Royal Navy during the war than either gunfire or torpedoes. This weapon, at which British admirals had been inclined to sneer, and which the Navy was ill prepared either to use or to combat, became a decisive factor in the war at sea. This book will endeavour to trace how an insignificant branch of the Royal Navy evolved to deal with the menace to British warships and merchantmen and how the Navy eventually learnt to use mines itself effectively against its enemies.

It should be mentioned here that mines were extensively used in other theatres of the war, including the Baltic, the Black Sea and the Mediterranean, but as the Royal Navy was not the main participant in laying or sweeping these minefields, they are not covered in this book. The exception is the Dardanelles – a mainly British operation that is covered in some detail.

CHAPTER 1

Origins

The idea of blowing up an enemy ship with some kind of explosive device is as old as gunpowder itself. The first successful attempt was in 1585 by the Dutch, who succeeded in blasting some Spanish ships using 'exploding boats', but these weapons cannot really be classified as 'mines' as they lacked one essential ingredient – they did not explode under water. A mine in the proper sense of the term must be a device intended to explode under water, where it can do maximum damage to its victim and where the surrounding water pressure makes the explosion more effective than it would be on the surface. Obviously, the construction of a true mine would have to await developments in engineering and of materials that were not available until the early stages of the industrial revolution of the eighteenth century.

The deployment of an underwater weapon was first attempted during the American War of Independence. It is significant that this was a situation in which a nation with a very weak naval power (the American revolutionaries) was attacking one with a strong navy (Britain). For many years thereafter the mine was regarded as the weapon of a weak power, and this was to lead to severe problems for the British in the future. It is important to point out at this stage that what we would call 'mines' were in the eighteenth and nineteenth century often called 'torpedoes' and torpedoes were sometimes called 'locomotive mines'. It is easier to understand accounts of warfare at that time if this is kept in mind.

The pioneer of mine warfare was an American called David Bushnell. His first attempt (September 1776) was against the British frigate *Eagle*, flagship of Lord Howe. He had devised a primitive submarine named the *Turtle*. *Turtle* was an egg-shaped device about six feet from top to bottom, which accommodated a single occupant, Ezra Lee, a sergeant. Lee had two screws that he turned by hand, one horizontal to give forward movement, and one vertical. There was also a rudder and a water pump to control ballast weight. Together these must have kept Lee pretty busy. A tiny conning tower projected above the water to enable Lee to see where he was. On the outside of the vessel was a magazine containing 150 lb of gunpowder. There was a screw attached to the magazine by a lanyard, and this was to be inserted into the enemy vessel, and a thirty-minute clock started; the clock would then detonate the magazine when *Turtle* had had a chance to get clear. *Turtle* was towed to a concealed point up tide of *Eagle*, which was lying in New York Harbour, close to Governor's Island. At first Lee was carried past *Eagle* by the tide, but he managed to get back to her and tried to insert the screw. It was impossible, however, to penetrate the copper sheathing around her hull. As daylight approached, the sergeant had to abandon his mission and released the magazine, which drifted away harmlessly. Lee escaped unhurt.

Bushnell made several more attempts against British shipping. One 'magazine' was launched against a frigate

Cerberus, but it missed her and struck a small schooner close by causing several casualties. He then adopted a much more promising tactic, this time drifting kegs of explosive slung below floating buoys down towards ships lying in the Delaware River. Unfortunately for the Americans the river was starting to freeze over at the time of launching, and this had caused the British to move their ships clear of the main stream, and out of the main path of the drifting kegs. Also the ice delayed the progress of the kegs down tide so that they arrived in daylight, not in the dark as intended. In daylight it was not difficult for the British to fend off any kegs getting near their ships, but one boat's crew, attempting to capture a keg, was insufficiently careful and it blew up killing four men and wounding others. Thus Bushnell's campaign came to an end without conclusive result.

In the French revolutionary wars an American citizen, Robert Fulton, made a number of attempts to interest both the French and the British Governments in a device that he had invented, not entirely unlike Bushnell's, for getting an explosive charge tethered to the hull of an enemy ship. The vehicle for delivering the mine, named *Nautilus*, was a copper-sheathed iron submarine, equipped with a sail for use on the surface and a hand-driven screw for underwater propulsion. Some successful trials were conducted, but both the British and the French considered the device 'dastardly' and did not use it. The British did, however, attempt to use 'explosive catamarans' proposed by Fulton, against the French fleet off Boulogne in 1804. These were not very successful, and the whole enterprise was considered rather unsporting. No such nice moral judgements were to apply in the savage total wars of the next century.

Fulton was not finished. In 1804 he came up with new proposals, including one for a moored mine that consisted of a brass case containing 100 lb of gunpowder with a firing pin on top. This was provided with buoyancy by cork. It had one entirely novel feature, which was a system for locking the firing pin after a pre-determined period so as to render the mine harmless. Thus, it had many of the characteristics of a twentieth century sea mine. It was never used in practice. Yet another Fulton development, made during the Anglo-American war of 1812, was a submersible vessel with a turtle-shaped metal shell designed to protrude slightly above the water. This towed a number of 'torpedoes' as it proceeded through an enemy anchorage. The 'torpedoes' were released and detonated as they struck enemy ships. One of these devices was captured by the British when it went aground on Long Island in 1814 and this appears to be the only one ever used in anger. Fulton died in 1815. His career as an armaments manufacturer was not notably successful, although some of his ideas formed the basis of subsequent successful developments. Interestingly, his motive was not money or even patriotism. He genuinely believed that his devices were so awful that they would make war at sea in future inconceivable to intelligent humans. A man of many parts, he was also a notable artist and a pioneer of steam-propelled boats.

At this point it is necessary to distinguish between different types of mine that would come into use in the nineteenth and twentieth centuries. These can be divided into the following general categories:

Ground mines

These are mines designed to sit on the seabed, typically to protect a harbour from enemy attack. These are frequently controlled from an observation station on shore and detonated when an enemy ship is in the act of entering the harbour.

Drifting mines

These are normally allowed to drift under the influence of tides or currents, in the way that Bushnell's kegs were used in the Delaware River. Drifting mines can also be released by a fleet fleeing from a superior enemy in the hope of destroying some of his ships. As we shall see, the British became very concerned about such tactics during the First World War.

Some quite ingenious drifting mines had been designed that creep up rivers on the rising tide and stay still on the ebb.

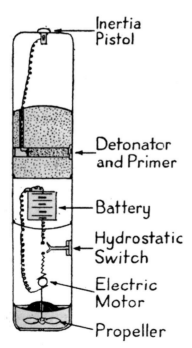

Inertia Pistol

Detonator and Primer

Battery

Hydrostatic Switch

Electric Motor

Propeller

Figure 1: A Leon mine. These were designed to drift free, with depth being maintained by an electric motor and hydrostat. When the battery was exhausted, they sunk to the bottom. In practice they were not much used, although the Royal Navy did sow some in the North Sea.

Normally, drifting mines have some sort of self-destruct device so that they do not constitute a permanent hazard to shipping.

A more elaborate type of drifting mine was known as the Leon mine (see Figure 1). This was a drifting mine designed to maintain a pre-set depth under water by means of a hydrostat and a small electric motor that actuated a vertical propeller, rotating in either direction so as to drive the mine either upwards or downwards. Leon mines could be launched into a harbour or anchorage and would drift towards an attacking enemy fleet, detonating when struck by a ship. They might also be dropped by a fleeing warship so as to threaten its pursuers, or so as to drift down tide towards an enemy fleet. They had a limited life and would sink harmlessly to the bottom when the battery ran out of power.

Moored mines

These are by far the most widely used type, and are moored to the sea bed by a cable. They can be detonated in a number of ways:

- By contact using a trigger mechanism outside the mine itself.
- By 'influence', either magnetic or sonic.
- By means of long whiskers or antennas projecting from the mine.
- By remote control by an observer on shore.

Normally, moored mines have a deactivating device that makes them safe if the mooring line should part.

Limpet mines

These are fixed to the hull of an enemy ship by frogmen or midget submarines.

After the Anglo-American war, the next use of mines in warfare was during the Schleswig-Holstein war of 1848–51 fought between Prussia and Denmark. Denmark had by far the most powerful fleet and the Prussians feared that they would use it to force their way into Kiel harbour. They employed a system of ground mines that could be set off by means of an electrical current from on shore. This had been devised by Professor Himmel of Kiel University – an early example of a 'boffin' being used to gain military advantage. The system was successful in that the Danish fleet was deterred from forcing an entry.

Much more extensive use of mines was made in the Crimean War (1854–6). Russia was at war with Britain, France and Turkey, and being the weaker power at sea, was active in employing mines to protect its harbours. Two types of mine were used. Ground mines detonated by observers on shore were employed, as well as moored contact mines containing 25 lb of gunpowder, which incorporated a most ingenious fuse that was to be the forerunner of the system used for many years almost universally. A glass tube was encased in a lead 'horn' that would bend as soon as it was contacted by a ship, breaking the glass tube. The broken tube would release the sulphuric acid that it contained into a mixture of potassium chlorate and sugar. This caused a small explosion, which in turn detonated the gunpowder. These were sometimes known as 'Nobel mines', after their inventor (the father of the famous Alfred Nobel) Immanuel Noble. At least two British ships were damaged by these mines when they attempted to approach the Russian base at Kronstadt in the course of the war. At the same time the Russians employed some large ground mines with electrical detonation. These do not appear to have been fired.

The American Civil War (1861–5) saw extensive use of mines mainly by the Confederates – again the weaker naval power. Many of the mines used were simple kegs of gunpowder, often laid in pairs with a friction device like a match head to fire them when they were struck. As an alternative, some were fitted with chemical fuses similar to the Russian horns. A more elaborate type of mine, the Singer mine, consisted of a metal cone filled with gunpowder, on top of which sat a heavy metal lid secured to a length of chain. These were tethered a little below the surface of the water. When a vessel hit the mine the lid was dislodged and fell off, jerking on the chain and setting off a friction fuse. The Singer mines were remarkable in that if the lid was knocked off by accident when the mine was being laid, a safety pin prevented the fuse from being activated. Another innovative development was known as 'The Devil Circumventor'. This was a mine designed to be laid in shallow rivers. It consisted of a case containing 100 lb of gunpowder, fitted with detonating horns. This was mounted on top of a spar, which in turn was connected to a universal joint on top of the anchor weight that held the whole device to the bottom, so that it stuck up rather like an underwater lollipop. Connected to the anchor was another mine sitting on the seabed, so that any attempt to sweep the device was sure to detonate the underwater mine. This was the first example of an anti-sweeping system. Ground mines were also employed by Confederate forces, one containing 1,000 lb of gunpowder and detonated electrically, successfully destroyed a powerful Federal gunboat.

No account of mining in the Civil War can be complete without mention of the use of towed mines or 'spar torpedoes'. Spar torpedoes were explosive devices mounted on long spars sticking out from the side of fast-moving steam launches or stealthy semi-submersible boats. These would be manoeuvred so that the mine on the end of the spar would strike the target and explode. A further development of the same principle consisted of a launch that would tow a mine behind it on the end of a long cable. The launch would then try to cut across the bows of a moving target so that the mine struck it. These weapons were extremely risky to those who used them and were to be rendered obsolete by the introduction of quick-firing secondary armament and self-propelled torpedoes. Nevertheless, they were employed by both sides and achieved some notable successes.

In all, twenty-two ships were destroyed by mines during the Civil War, and many more severely damaged. The mine had decidedly come of age.

Two final nineteenth century wars saw a further significant development in mining technology. The Austro-Prussian war of 1866 saw the development of the Hertz horn, which was first incorporated in German mines during this conflict (see Figure 2). The Hertz horn was to become a feature of the vast majority of contact mines used in both world wars. It consisted of a lead horn containing a glass tube similar to the Russian mines described above, however in this case, instead of a chemical reaction, the fuse acted electrically. Breaking the glass tube released a bichromate solution onto two plates, one zinc, the other carbon. This immediately constituted a battery and generated an electrical current that passed to a

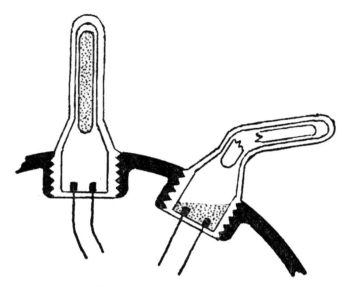

Figure 2: The Hertz horn. A ship striking the soft lead horn bends it and breaks a glass tube inside, which allows acid to contact two electrodes, setting up a battery that immediately generates a current detonating the mine. By far the most satisfactory system for detonating contact mines.

platinum wire bridge embedded in fulminate of mercury; the current fused the bridge and ignited the priming composition, which in turn fired the main charge. This elegant device acted almost instantaneously and proved reliable and long lasting in service. Mines fitted with Hertz horns protected German harbours against the greatly superior French fleet in the Franco-Prussian war of 1870 and thereafter the German Navy paid great attention to the manufacture and deployment of moored mines.

In the Russo-Japanese war of 1904–1905, mines were to prove a decisive weapon. The Russian Pacific Fleet was bottled up in Port Arthur. Russia was at the time probably the world leader in mine design and manufacture, having successfully used them in the Crimean war and in the subsequent Russo Turkish war. By 1904, Russian mines used either the Nobel or the Hertz firing systems and were filled with guncotton instead of gunpowder. They were mostly conical in structure with a single horn projecting out of a domed top.

Japanese mines drew the first blood, however. At first, the Japanese had failed to obtain decisive results by attacking the Russian fleet in harbour using torpedo boats. These did no great damage but seem to have demoralized the Russian Navy so that it did not interfere with Japanese troop landings behind the town. The supine performance of the Russian Navy prompted the selection of a more aggressive commander. Vice Admiral Stepan Makaroff was dispatched to Port Arthur and immediately breathed new life into the fleet. The Japanese, however, decided to lay mines in the region of the port. These were moored contact mines detonated by a pendulum. The Russians appear to have seen these being laid, but forgot about them in the heat of battle. On 13 April, Makaroff took his five battleships to sea to support an action between his own destroyers and the enemy. When the Japanese battle fleet appeared he retired, hoping to draw the Japanese ships into range of his coastal artillery. As he neared the coast his ship *Petropavlovsk* struck a mine and was lost, together with the Admiral and most of the crew. A few minutes later a similar fate befell another battleship, *Pobieda*; she stayed afloat, however, and was towed home. Russia had lost the one commander who might have won the war. This was an early example of a new tactic developed by the Japanese – offensive mine laying close to an enemy coast.

On 15 May the tables were turned when the captain of a Russian minelayer managed to observe the normal course taken by blockading Japanese forces outside Port Arthur and two Japanese battleships *Yashima* and *Hatsuse* blundered into a minefield that he cunningly laid in their path, sinking one and severely damaging the other. A little later two Japanese cruisers suffered the same fate. The Japanese had attempted to sweep part of the minefield and mark the unswept area with buoys, but the Russians, some of whose junior officers seem to have shown a degree of aggression and resourcefulness that shamed their superiors, had cunningly moved the Japanese marker buoys. Although this impressive success gave the Russians an opportunity to seize the initiative, deprived of their bold leader, they did not take it and stayed in harbour where their ships ended up being destroyed by the artillery of the advancing Japanese Army. Such was the ignoble end of the Russian Pacific Fleet. During the campaign they had laid 4,275 mines and these sunk two battleships, two cruisers, five gunboats six destroyers and a dispatch ship – a far greater haul than they achieved by all other weapons combined. The Russians themselves lost one battleship, one cruiser, two destroyers, a torpedo boat and a gunboat to mines. The war concluded with the attempt by the Russian Baltic Fleet to intervene and its subsequent crushing defeat at Tsushima. Things might have turned out differently if Makaroff had been in command at Port Arthur.

CHAPTER 2

Mines and the Royal Navy

British observers had, of course, watched the development of mines but the Royal Navy, by far the largest and best equipped in the world, had been able to reach no conclusion regarding how it should react. At first, mines were regarded as nasty, sneaky devices, which might be used by to protect a fleet anchorage from surprise attack, but which had no other purpose. Wider use of mines would tend to obstruct the fleet when manoeuvring at sea, and equally importantly would hamper the vitally important merchant service that carried Britain's overseas trade. Britain as the dominant sea power, it was argued, would be mad to do anything that restricted movement of ocean-going vessels. Mines were not ignored entirely, however, and the main fleet harbours were protected by a system of defensive mines installed, rather surprisingly, not by the Navy but by the Royal Engineers. The mines were of two types:

i) Observation mines containing 500 lb of gun cotton. A line of these would be laid across the harbour mouth. They were fired from on shore by hidden observers equipped with telescopes mounted on swivels, normally working from two observation stations. The telescopes would be pointed at the attacking ship and would follow it as it approached the harbour. An electrical contact would be made when the angle of the two telescopes indicated that the ship was over the mine, and the mine would fire. If the entrance to the harbour was narrow a single telescope was sufficient.

ii) Contact mines containing 76 lb of guncotton. These were contact mines fitted with a detonator fired electrically by anything that struck the mine, due to the displacement of mercury in a tube or an inertia weight. They were connected to a base on shore so that the mines would normally be in an inactivated condition, but would be set to 'active' when enemy ships were expected.

The Navy considered that such mine defences were a useful adjunct to gun defences, and adopted a training regime under which officers and men were instructed in how to lay mine defences across temporary fleet anchorages without the help of the Army. At the same time a system of countermining was developed. A launch would lay a string of small mines as close as possible to an enemy defensive minefield and detonate them electrically. The explosion of these small mines would set off the enemy defensive mines and thus destroy the defences of the enemy harbour. It would have required pretty cool nerves on the part of the crew of the launch to carry out such an operation in practice.

At the same time, consideration was given to the problems of mooring offensive and defensive mines. A mine must be positioned below the surface of the sea, and must remain there whatever the state of the tide or weather. Its depth will vary according to the state of the tide and the strength of the currents, which will cause it to pull on the mooring rope and tend to drag it deeper in the water. Laid too deep, a mine is obviously ineffective; too shallow and it will be above water at low tide and thus easy to avoid and destroy. This meant that early mine laying operations had to know exactly where each individual mine would be moored and the mooring cable would be cut to length, taking into account tidal range and current. Obviously, this was highly inconvenient and the problem was presented to HMS *Vernon*, the torpedo school at Portsmouth. This establishment was responsible for torpedo and wireless development as well as mines and attracted some of the best brains in the Navy. Unfortunately, mines were at this stage the 'poor relation' in *Vernon*'s activities and this would lead to severe problems in 1914, but the mooring issue was elegantly resolved by one of the staff, Lieutenant Ottley. Ottley's device, known as the 'Plummet System' (see Figure 3), comprised a mooring cable for the mine mounted on a rotating drum inside the mooring weight. When the mine is dropped it remains floating on the surface, while the mooring weight sinks towards the bottom, unreeling the cable as it does so. Suspended beneath the mooring weight is a plummet on the end of a line whose length is the desired depth of the mine beneath the water. When the plummet hits the bottom the tension on this line is released, and this in turn locks the drum so that as the mooring weight continues its journey to the seabed it hauls the mine down after it to the set depth. The length of the plummet line can be adjusted according to the tidal state at the moment of laying and the local tidal range.

While the Plummet System was reasonably satisfactory, a more accurate arrangement was eventually developed

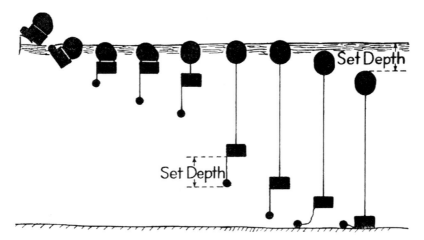

Figure 3: The plummet system of mooring. The mine and the mooring are released together, and the plummet wire starts to descend as soon as the mine is clear of the wash of the minelayer. The plummet dangles below the mine, the length of the wire holding it being the depth at which the mine will be below the surface of the water at the particular state of tide prevailing when the mine is laid. When the plummet strikes the bottom it locks the reel on which the mine's mooring cable is wound so that the mine is dragged down to the required depth by the mooring weight. Before the mines are laid, the correct length of plummet wire has to be selected, taking into account the depth of water and the state of tide. The system could also be used to lay deep mines to catch submarines.

incorporating a hydrostat. In this system the mine and the mooring weight are dropped together and sink to the bottom. After a set time a soluble plug dissolves and the mine is released and rises towards the surface, unreeling the mooring cable inside it as it does so. At a depth determined by the setting of the hydrostat, the reel is locked and the mine is ready. An alternative system allowed the reel to be mounted within the mooring weight. In this case the

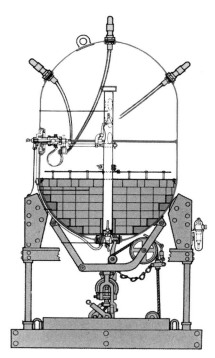

Figure 4: A German 'egg' mine of the type used by surface ships. The mine and sinker are dropped together and when the sinker has settled on the bottom the mine is released and floats upward, unreeling a double length of wire as it does so. When the mine reaches the required depth a hydrostat within it actuates a cable clamp. Hertz horns are used to fire the mine. The mine is moored by two wires, which tends to cause it to swing about too much in a tideway; otherwise this is an excellent design.

mooring line would be double and the hydrostat within the mine would lock the cable as it passed through a pulley wheel at the base of the mine. This system was used on German 'egg mines' (see Figure 4).

The Admiralty, however, remained doubtful about the value of mines, and in 1903 took the decision to cease to deploy independent mines altogether. Mines were, according to official opinion, ineffective in preventing attack by torpedo boats on a fleet in harbour, and the increased range and accuracy of heavy guns made them unnecessary.

The lessons of the Russo-Japanese war soon forced the Admiralty to change its tune. *Vernon* was once again

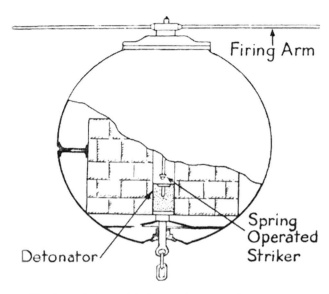

Figure 5: The British Naval Spherical Mine. This type was adopted in 1905. Contact with the firing arm released the striker and fired the mine. In practice, these were very unsatisfactory, frequently refusing to explode and coming adrift.

ordered to produce a workable independent mine. In 1905, 1,000 'Naval Spherical Mines' were ordered (see Figure 5). These were spheres filled with guncotton with horizontal firing arms on top, which when struck by a ship triggered a mechanical striker. They were fitted with the plummet system to control depth. The mechanical trigger system was selected because the Navy had a strong if ill-founded objection to electrics at sea and thus considered the Hertz horns unreliable. Another factor was cost. A mine fitted with Hertz horns was estimated to cost £200 – twice the price of the selected design. They also rejected pendulum or mercury-operated detonators because these had a tendency to be triggered by rough seas. In practice, the Naval Spherical mine proved very unsatisfactory, often failing to explode when struck. At the same time, all the old observation mines and electro-mechanical defensive mines were withdrawn. There must have been an audible sigh of relief among junior officers detailed to man launches when the explosive counter-mining tactic for disposing of enemy mines was abolished in 1907.

Enemy mines had to be countered, however, and some effort was put into devising a satisfactory means of sweeping them. The simplest device was a cable, dragged between two ships, kept underwater by weights. This was most unsatisfactory as it depended on the ships keeping exactly the correct distance apart to avoid the sweep dragging on the bottom or coming out of the water. A study of systems used by fishing trawlers resulted in a proposal for an 'otter' or 'kite' that would maintain the sweep at a constant depth between two vessels. A lot of work was put into developing kites and eventually a satisfactory arrangement was devised in which each vessel towed a kite, attached to the ship's winch, which remained at a selected depth under water depending on forward speed and the length of the tow rope (see Figure 6). It was so designed that it maintained position almost directly in line with the towing ship's track. The kite was a substantial structure weighing about one ton. A sweeping line about 500 yards long was streamed between the two kites, passing through a ring in the corner of the kites. The sweeping line itself was normally a two-and-a–half-inch cable. Initially, a standard cable was used, but eventually, in 1916, a serrated cable that would cut through the mooring line more effectively, using a sawing action, was introduced. This worked even if the sweeper was moving

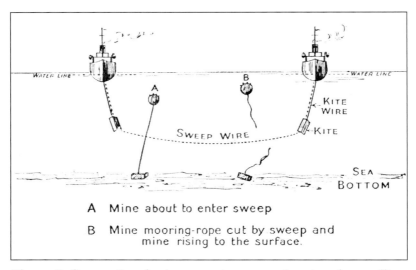

A Mine about to enter sweep

B Mine mooring-rope cut by sweep and
   mine rising to the surface.

Figure 6: Conventional minesweeping gear – two trawlers pulling kites. The length of the kite wire and the speed of the trawlers determine the depth of the sweep wire between them. The sweep wire would typically be about 500 yards long. Serrated wires came into use during the war so as to improve the chance of cutting through the mooring, otherwise the mine and its sinker had to be towed into shallow water before it could be destroyed.

quite slowly. With luck the sweeping line would part the mine's mooring cable so that the mine would then rise to the surface to be disposed of by gunfire. At first rifles were used, these might either explode the mine if a horn was hit, or might hole it and sink it. Later, sweepers were issued with deck guns and even machine guns for the purpose. Frequently, the mooring line would not part and the mine would be dragged along until the sinker became detached, or the mine reached shallow enough water to be clearly visible and could thus be destroyed.

There were at this stage no purpose-built minesweepers. To

protect the battle fleet at sea moderately fast vessels were needed and for this purpose outdated gunboats or old destroyers manned by regular naval personnel were pressed into service. At the outbreak of the war the fast minesweeping fleet was commanded by Commander Preston, who was to prove an extremely able officer. He remained in minesweeping activities throughout the war, finishing up as Director of Minesweeping at the Admiralty. The little ships had a torrid time of it in the early months, steaming ahead of the fleet. Unlike more recent destroyers these were all coal burners, and the furnaces had to be fed by men with shovels, working in an incredibly confined space, as they struggled to keep station ahead of the fleet. The brief periods of rest they had in port were invariably interrupted by the filthy process of coaling. Often, their range was so short when steaming at the required speed of twelve knots that they had to set out with a deck cargo of coal. It soon became clear that the fast sweepers needed to be supplemented, and for this civilian vessels had to be recruited. These were fast railway packets, larger and with much longer endurance than the ancient warships. They were frequently used to sweep in dangerous waters close to the enemy coast, to make sure that there was a safe area in which elements of the Grand Fleet could manoeuvre or destroyers could carry out raids. Altogether, the fast minesweeping force had a demanding and dangerous task.

It was also anticipated that it might be necessary to sweep offensive enemy mines laid close to British harbours or in shipping lanes. To achieve this an original approach was taken. Admiral Lord Charles Beresford, Commander of the Home Fleet, visited the Humber in 1907 to follow up a suggestion that commercial fishermen might be capable of using their trawlers and drifters to perform this function. He was impressed by their seamanship and skills in handling heavy gear at sea and reported favourably. Thus, the Royal Naval Minesweeping Reserve (RNMR) was formed. The men received some training but were not under naval discipline and did not wear uniform. They were under the control of their regular skippers, who normally went to sea wearing a bowler hat and a tweed suit, which was adorned with Navy-issue brass buttons, of which they were extremely proud. The deckhands were regular English and Scots east coast fishermen. In those days it took six years before a boy going to sea on a trawler became qualified as a regular hand, so the level of seamanship and ship handling skills of these hands was extremely high – they had much more seagoing experience than most naval ratings. As the war went on and the urgency of the mine issue increased, more and more naval officers and petty officers found themselves posted to the minesweeping service.

The navigational methods used by trawlermen were, to say the least, unorthodox. In the days of radio and satellite assisted navigation it is easy to forget what an inexact science this was in the early twentieth century. Experienced navigators on warships were often fifteen or twenty miles out in their dead reckoning estimates after a couple of days at sea. If cloud cover was thick there was no way of checking one's position by sun or star sights. Men who had been fishing the North Sea all their lives, however, simply knew where they were. The only instrument most of the little ships used was a compass, and the forefathers of the RNMR skippers would probably have regarded that as a bit of an effeminate gadget. If you were a North Sea fisherman and didn't develop some sort of sixth sense for direction finding, you didn't last long. One Royal Navy officer described the achievements of a trawler skipper attached to his command. Often, the trawler had to separate from the rest of the flotilla and rendezvous later at some convenient spot in the North Sea. Whenever he was ordered to do this the trawler skipper asked for a bearing from Lowestoft. Given this, he never failed to appear on time at the right place, although he had little idea of charts or instruments. A bearing from Lowestoft was all he needed to find his way to any spot in the North Sea. An amusing incident is recorded from a minesweeper working out of Granton in a thick fog that had persisted for several days. The naval officer in command was unsure of his position until a deckhand caught a glimpse of a small boat through the fog. 'We're fifteen miles nor'east of St Abb's Head,' sang out the deckhand. 'Rubbish', replied the Captain 'We're nowhere near there.' 'I can't help where you think we are,' was the reply. 'But that's old Andy MacPherson in that boat and he's been shooting a line of lobster pots 'ere these forty years'. He was right, of course.

Two types of fishing boat were used. Most of the sweeping was done by steam trawlers; these were steel-built coal-burning vessels of 200–300 tons and about 110–140 feet long, with 13 foot draft. Top speed was 9–11 knots. Typically, they would have a crew of twelve. Accustomed to fishing as far afield as the coasts of North Africa and the Arctic Sea, they were fine sea boats. As the war progressed, many of them were fitted with 6-pounder quick-firing guns to sink mines and to ward off U-boats. There were many instances of them proving extremely aggressive in service. One of the first U-boat sinkings of the war was achieved by Skipper Youngston of the *Dorothy Grey*. He used his trawler to ram his victim, which had attempted to enter Scapa Flow. He damaged her hydroplanes so badly that she became uncontrollable and drifted through the Pentland Skerries firing distress signals. Most of her crew were rescued by a gunboat before the submarine sank in the turbulent waters. Youngston and his crew were awarded £500 by the Admiralty and a further £100 was given to another trawler, *Tokio*, which had assisted in the chase. On another occasion later in the war some trawlers were escorting a slow convoy back from Ireland. All of a sudden there was a disturbance in the water and a 'huge' submarine appeared and opened fire (she was actually probably one of the U.139 class of cruiser submarines, of 2,000 tons surface displacement mounting two 5.9-inch guns and with a surface speed of 16 knots). Following the lead of their commanding officer in *Conan Doyle*, the trawlers formed into line of battle like so many ships of the line and returned the fire with their puny armament. The submarine closed the range, with her heavy guns and high speed she should have had little difficulty in dealing with a handful of lightly armed fishing boats. One of them, *Asne*, was badly hit and suffered one man killed and four wounded, but the unequal battle continued. The trawlers began to run short of ammunition and *Conan Doyle* signalled 'Prepare to ram.' It was not necessary. A lucky shot from the second trawler in line knocked the submarine's forward gun over the side, damaging the hull in the process. The powerful vessel decided she had had enough and dived suddenly. It was never determined whether or not she survived.

British trawlers were joined as the war went on by increasing numbers of captured German fishing boats and by various Scandinavian and even Spanish trawlers purchased by the Admiralty for war service. These were manned by naval and RNMR crews.

The other type of fishing boat used were the drifters, designed to shoot and then ride to drift nets. These were mostly wooden steam boats, but some had oil engines. They had a steadying sail to hold them into wind when riding to nets. Drifters were slower than the trawlers and had a shallower draft. They were normally used for laying marker buoys to define the limits of minefields or for other auxiliary duties.

Trawlers worked in groups of six to twelve vessels, each group being under control of a Royal Navy officer – frequently from the Royal Naval Reserve (RNR), or Royal Naval Volunteer Reserve (RNVR). RNR officers were in some cases retired regular naval men, and sometimes volunteers from the Merchant Navy. The RNVR were mostly yachtsmen volunteers. They were something of figures of fun among their regular colleagues. On one occasion an RNVR officer unwisely picked up a small shell that had been fired at his ship and had failed to explode. 'By golly it's hot!' he yelled as it burnt his hands before dropping it. For the rest of the war, whenever one of the crew met an RNVR officer they would start the conversation with 'By golly it's hot.' Relationships between fishing boat skippers and the naval officers they worked with seem to have been generally excellent, at least in British coastal waters.

A few weeks after the outbreak of war some 200 fishing vessels were enrolled in the RNMR, and many more joined as the conflict took its course. Normal fishing activities were, of course, very much restricted by the war, and skippers were often glad of the assured income minesweeping service provided. Flotillas of RNMR sweepers were initially based on The Nore, Harwich, Lowestoft, The Humber, The Tyne, and Granton in the Firth of Forth. Eventually, they spread to cover the whole of the British Isles.

This motley fleet was put under the command of Rear Admiral Ned Charlton, Ned was installed in a succession of requisitioned steam yachts, and was frequently actively engaged in sweeping operations himself. He was popular with his men but not with Admiral Fisher, the First Sea Lord, who considered him an incompetent muddler. Fisher wrote to Jellicoe on 21 May 1915, with typical over statement.

Minesweeping is really the one chief thing in the war and in view of the certainty (now very near us) of every yard of the North Sea being infested with mines, Charlton is quite unfit for so immense a job and Madden is the ONLY man.

However, Charlton lasted in his post longer than Fisher himself, as Ned Charlton remained in command of mine-sweeping until October 1916, when he was transferred to command the Cape of Good Hope. Fisher resigned in May 1915. One incident that he recorded gives a good picture of early sweeping operations:

I was engaged in looking after the sweepers in a yacht manned throughout by RNR and RNVR officers, most of whom were undergraduates from Cambridge. It was a misty day and mines, we were led to believe, had been laid in the fairway. While searching we observed a mine blow up alongside a steamer about a mile away to the northward. Fortunately for us perhaps we were heading south east and had to turn round to close her. Between us and the steamer was a patrol trawler heading north. Without the slightest hesitation this little vessel made a bee-line for the disabled ship which we could see was in a bad way with one of the boats hanging vertically from the davits. When the trawler got within 150 yards of her there was a terrific explosion and the trawler's stern cocked up in the air and her still revolving propellers had disappeared under water before the pieces had stopped falling. We stopped at once and picked up seven survivors. We observed the bulky form of a man floating on the surface with his head under water. The bow wash seemed to dislodge some air out of his clothing and his body disappeared, a man in our bows immediately dived in after him and both were hauled on board together. The unconscious man was treated by our doctor but I regret to say his efforts were of no avail. The man turned out to be the mate, and a fisherman, and left a widow and eleven children.

Such were the experiences of the Rear Admiral. He, in fact, managed to persuade the Admiralty to count RNMR sailors as naval personnel when they were killed or injured in action, like this poor mate, and their families were, thanks to his efforts, awarded a full naval pension.

Signalling was obviously very important to minesweepers and to the ships they were working to protect. Naval minesweepers all had radio, but the fishing boats did not. Initially, the lead boat in each group only was issued with a radio, and operators were hastily trained, some being boy sailors who volunteered from training ships. Their most critical duty was sending out 'Q' messages. These were instituted by Charlton immediately after the loss of *Audacious*. Had this procedure been in place earlier, the *Manchester Commerce* mine strike would have been known and reported immediately and the battleship might not have been lost. Q messages were top-priority messages sent to all ships as soon as a new minefield was located, or a merchant ship struck a mine. Action was then taken to divert or hold all traffic and call up the nearest sweepers.

Inexperienced radio officers caused some amusing incidents:

Trawler *Columba* to minesweeper HQ: 'Being shelled by submarine and bombed by aeroplane.'

HQ immediately sent a relief party of a destroyer and an armed yacht and wirelessed *Columba* repeatedly but got no answer.

Eventually, *Columba* was located none the worse. The submarine had disappeared and the aeroplane had been shot at with rifles by almost all the crew and had flown away.

Relief party: What are you doing?
Columba: Picking up fish killed by bomb explosion.
Relief party: Why didn't you answer my signals?
Columba: Wireless operator collecting fish.

As we shall see in the narrative many new types of minesweeper came into service as the war progressed, and new techniques were developed, but the east coast trawlers with their fisherman crews continued to bear the brunt of the work. No fewer than 250 were lost during the war, 214 of these to mines.

An illustration of the work of a trawlerman who joined the RNMR is provided by Skipper John Harwood. He related his story.

I joined up at about the beginning of 1915, and had been trawl fishing before then. At this time we had to produce two years' deep sea fishing discharges before they would have us; but it wasn't very long after that practically anyone could wangle their way onto the sweepers.

I left Aberdeen on board the trawler *Rose IV*, official number 1183. I was over eighteen months in her and I believe it was about my happiest time in the whole war... our orders were for Holyhead, but the funny thing was there wasn't a soul on aboard who knew where Holyhead was.

About Christmas 1916 we were sent to Portland. I was signalman at the time. We were put on to patrolling off the Casquets (a group of rocks close to the Channel Islands). My word but we had some weather to contend with. We worked fourteen days out and seven in. From Portland we were sent to Pompey, and then we really knew what trawlers were doing.

We were put into a section of sweepers and used to sweep daily between the Owers and the Nab lightship. One day we were sweeping and got seven mines laid by a German submarine. Seven again next day in exactly the same place. A third day we were getting them again when a signalman in our opposite number the *Apley* sent me a signal 'This is the last lap for England home and beauty. Give her hell!' meaning get some more power into our sweeping. Then BANG! Off goes a mine under our port quarter which parted our sweep wire and kite wire. The *Apley* was blown up a few weeks later and there were only two or three survivors.

Then we were put on the French coal transport (France's industry and economy were dependent on British coal throughout the war), and went to France with convoys every night. It was just a case of hell for leather all the time from St Helen's to Le Havre. It was a monotonous job tho' submarines were active and took a fair toll.

Harwood then was promoted to second hand – effectively, mate of a trawler – and sent off to Alexandria where he joined the trawler *Margaret Duncan* whose skipper was an ex-skipper of a large private yacht. 'A proper little toff,' Harwood called him. After working on various convoy missions, Harwood was kept busy sweeping Turkish mines off the coasts of Syria and Lebanon. Some of these had been laid in the tideless waters only about two feet below the surface. They had to be buoyed by parties in rowing boats, who could see them under the water (and had to be careful how they rowed, an oar dug too deep could easily detonate a mine). Once marked the mines could be swept by trawlers, a drifter bringing up the rear destroying them by gunfire. This work continued some time after the war was over. When the job was complete the little ships were sent home. The drifters with them were in poor shape, their engines practically worn out, so they had to be towed by trawlers much of the way – a slow and dangerous operation.

All in all, an eventful and exciting war for a fisherman, who was soon back at his trade as master of the Aberdeen trawler *Hannah E Reynolds*.

The east coast of England was an even more active area as far as minesweeping was concerned. This is well illustrated by the activities of Chief Skipper Martin Fielding RNR.

When the war broke out he was serving as mate on a trawler, working close to the Amrun Bank lightship, in an area much frequented by the German Navy. They concentrated on finding soles and turbot and took little notice of the warships charging about nearby. Fielding himself, however, was surreptitiously reading Erskine Childers' *Riddle of the Sands* whenever he got an opportunity. One night they noticed that the lightship had been extinguished and they decided to fish elsewhere. This was lucky because the light went out on the day war was declared and many British trawlers in the area were swept up by the Germans and their crews interned for the duration. Fielding got his call-up papers as soon as his boat got home and served for a time on a cruiser and in various shore-based posts then got his posting as first mate in a minesweeping trawler.

> Three days afterwards I saw my first mine floating near the mouth of the Humber. Three or four sweepers stopped to sink it by rifle fire, and several of our men were on the bridge watching their efforts. Although warned not to get closer than 200 yards, our ships were gradually drifting nearer as the mine seemed to have a charmed life. Suddenly it became covered in flame like a Christmas pudding. It looked quite pretty. – Crash! – Three of us in the wheelhouse were almost knocked off our feet. We hadn't seen a mine go up before, and for a moment we thought it was an earthquake, or the heavens had dropped.

Fielding was transferred to the paddle sweeper *Fair Maid* in October 1916. He continues his story:

> Broken sweep wires were at first a great trial to the fishermen. They became foul of the sea bottom or carried away because of bad station keeping. I can remember having to splice a wire as many as six times in six hours. The majority of fishermen had never spliced a wire and some thought a knot would do, but this was too dangerous

as it could catch in the mine mooring. I have seen faces and hands badly scratched and lacerated in the process of splicing. Soon the fishermen were able do it in six minutes.

It was soon evident that paddle sweepers were just the ideal vessels for use in shallow water owing to their light draft; also, they were faster than trawlers and covered more ground. Their disadvantages were they were no use in rough weather, they had pretty heavy coal consumption, and if lost they were more costly and difficult to replace. The casualties, too, were heavier than trawlers, for the paddlers had a crew of forty or fifty.

Fair Maid had very few fishermen. We had quite a mixture of merchant seamen and youths who hadn't seen much sea service. Up anchor early one morning and away to the Cross Sands light-ship. I had occasion to correct one of the seamen for not turning up at his post at the proper time. This led to a bit of cursing and swearing, the discipline of some of our men not being all that it should be. The time was about 8 am. Then fate took a hand – just a dull booming crash… then reality struck, I opened my eyes and I was under water. I felt as if my lungs would burst. I was trapped amongst wires and wreckage. I kicked and struggled, and it seemed an eternity before I reached the surface. How far down I was I don't know, but it seemed a long way. On the surface men were screaming and shouting. The *Fair Maid* seemed to be about 100 yards away almost broken in two, but still afloat and upright. I was always a strong swimmer and tried to make for the ship but found I couldn't move my right leg. It was numbed like cramp: it was freezing at the time and little did I think that I had been badly hurt. Boats were being lowered from the *Duchess of Buccleuch* and *Devonia* and other paddle sweepers. My eyes were getting dimmed; I was unknowingly bleeding to death. Eventually by a superhuman effort I got alongside *Fair Maid*.

In the event the cold water and an incredibly tough constitution saved his life in spite of a horrific loss of blood from deep wounds in the lower part of his body. After a period in hospital he was off sweeping again, this time as skipper of the trawler *Earl of Buchan*. On his first voyage in her he swept a large number of mines off Sheringham. He admitted to being in a nervous condition after his experience on *Fair Maid*. This was made worse when he found himself temporarily in charge of a group of sweepers and had to lead his charges into Lowestoft in a pea-soup fog. On a subsequent voyage, this time as skipper of the trawler *Strathmory*, he had another nasty experience. Mines were reported in the channel outside Yarmouth Roads. *Strathmory* was busily sweeping when the lead trawler blew up just in front of them, although luckily no one was killed. A little later he was sweeping with his partner boat *Coadjutor* close at hand.

> We felt a pull on the sweep wire and when this happened we generally increased speed if possible and by slackening and heaving in cut through the mine mooring wire. Only one ship could do this and that was the 'B boat' – *Coadjutor*. So I kept my course and speed and hoisted the signal 'Mine in sweep'. But *Coadjutor* was dropping astern and getting outside her distance. I signalled to increase speed. This he apparently couldn't do, so I had to equalize my speed with his to prevent the mine from running along the sweep wire towards him and blowing him up. Looking

through my glasses I saw great activity on *Coadjutor* people running forward etc so I signalled by semaphore 'What's wrong?' He replied 'The mine is in the kite'. Now this was a dangerous position. They had apparently slacked away all their kite wire in an effort to clear it but the chain and the moorings of the mine were foul of the chains on the kite. Had the mine exploded in that position nothing on earth could have saved her and the skipper had sent all his crew forward, leaving one hand on the winch.

Luckily, this time the mine somehow cleared itself and shot up into the air like a rubber ball, leaving its detonator stuck in the sweeping gear. Fielding was later hauled over the coals for sinking the mine instead of recovering it for the experts to take a look. He found this hard because he had had no way of knowing that the detonator had come out.

Asked what the bravest thing he had seen was Fielding referred to an incident when he had been in the sweeper *Vindelicia* in 1915. They had swept what seemed to be a new type of mine (it was probably one of the submarine laid variety) near Flamborough Head. It was bitterly cold, but volunteers were called for to capture the mine. A boat was lowered and two men, one stripped naked, made for the mine. The naked man dived into the water and worked on the mine with a marlin spike and some other tools, cutting wires and unscrewing threaded plugs. After a long, bitter struggle the fuse came out and the man returned almost dead with cold. The weapon was safely picked up and brought ashore.

Apart from their work of minesweeping, trawlers found themselves pressed into service in the role of guardians of the battle fleet. When Scapa and Cromarty were sufficiently well protected to be considered safe fleet anchorages, most of the gaps between the islands and rocks forming the atoll had been blocked by sunken blockships and barges. Controlled ground mines were positioned to trap any enemy sub or destroyer trying to sneak into the anchorage. Huge nets and mined obstructions were placed across the entrances used by the fleet. These, of course, had to be guarded and opened and closed as required by the warships and for this job trawlers were pressed into service. At first, this may not sound an arduous task, but the weather in the northern islands made it an incredibly tough billet. In the first winter of the war, exceptionally heavy gales with winds of 100 miles per hour swept the Flow and battleships rode there with steam up in case they dragged and two anchors streamed. Even in the shelter of the anchorage itself boats could not be launched to pass between ships. Outside the sheltered water, exposed to the full fury of the gale, rode the little trawlers, watching over the entrances and their defences, often only a few hundred yards off the terrible rocks. They depended on their primitive steam engines to hold them in position, and on their trusty stokers to keep those engines going. It is difficult today to conceive the conditions those crews faced, without respite, throughout the war.

Such were the wartime activities of the fishermen who kept the sea lanes open and defended the fleet anchorages throughout the war.

CHAPTER 3

German Mine Laying and the British Response

The Hague convention of 1907 limited the danger to merchant shipping and neutrals from mines, in theory. The main provisions were:

- Any unanchored mine must become harmless after one hour.
- Anchored mines must automatically become harmless if they break loose.
- No mines to be laid off enemy coasts with the intention of intercepting commercial traffic.
- Every precaution to be taken to ensure the safety of peaceful navigation.
- Mines to be removed at the end of the conflict.
- All mines not conforming to regulations to be converted so as to conform.

This was obviously an extremely badly constructed document (how, for example could one determine the intention behind the laying of a mine?) but it was accepted by most of the naval powers. Except insofar as they applied to deactivating mines that broke loose, Germany took little notice of the provisions at the outbreak of the war and none at all as it progressed. In mitigation, the Germans argued, quite legitimately, that the convention only came into effect if all the belligerents had signed it. Russia was a belligerent and had not signed so it was invalid. As the weaker naval power, and the nation least dependent on maritime trade, the German Navy saw the mine as a weapon that could inflict severe damage on its enemies. The North Sea, shallow, turbulent and opaque was a perfect environment for mining and constituted a highway for British shipping both naval and civilian. German strategy was designed to make the most of the potential of her mine laying capability from the outset.

German naval vessels were mostly equipped to lay mines if required, to protect a withdrawal for example, but there were no specialist minelayers, so the burden of the mine-laying effort had to be borne by requisitioned merchant ships and ferries. Germany had a large stock of very efficient mines of the Hertz horn type ready for the outbreak of war (see Figure 2). No time was lost in getting mining operations under way.

During the first days of August 1914, even before Britain declared war, the hastily converted North German Lloyd fast mail steamer *Königin Luise* put to sea with a cargo of 180 mines. Just before the outbreak of hostilities she had been re-painted so as to resemble a Great Eastern Railways ferry. She was unlucky enough to be spotted by a fishing boat 'throwing things over the side' some thirty miles off Southwold in the main shipping channel. The fishermen managed to get a message passed to the destroyer *Laurel*, which was nearby, and formed part of a patrol of destroyers out of Harwich accompanied by the light cruiser *Amphion*.

The weather was thick but the destroyers managed to get a sight of the intruder at 11.00 hours and very soon the destroyer *Lance* fired the first shot of the war at sea, using her 4-inch main armament. *Amphion* soon came up and joined in the firing with her 6-inch guns so that by noon *Königin Luise* was lying on her side, a helpless wreck. Her crew, who were partly naval and partly civilian, abandoned ship and 56 out of 130 of them were rescued. Many of the survivors were confined to a compartment in the bows of *Amphion* so that 'if we go on a mine you go first'. It was now a question of picking a way back to Harwich without running over the minefield. The voyage was interrupted by another suspicious vessel in Great Eastern Railways colours, but flying a large German ensign. Just as they were about to open fire on her, the ensign came down and an urgent message was flashed explaining that she was indeed a British ship and was transporting the German ambassador home following the declaration of war. The German ensign had been hoisted to guard against attack by German ships as she approached the coast. After this incident, *Amphion* continued on her way only to strike one mine, shortly followed by another. The ship was utterly destroyed, with pieces being hurled high into the air. Some 132 British officers and men were killed as well as 27 German prisoners. Many others were badly hurt.

At this point it is interesting to consider a first-hand account of what it was like to be on a ship running onto a mine while in action. This particular incident occurred in the last stages of the war, in May 1918. British forces had attempted to block the German-held harbour mouth at Zeebrugge. The operation met with partial success and the Navy was now determined to block Ostend also. The operation was commanded by Rear Admiral Roger Keyes. It was known that the harbour mouth was heavily defended by mines and gun emplacements, and British intelligence had learnt that nine powerful German destroyers had been moved to a position just outside Zeebrugge so as to intervene if another attempt to block the entrance any of the Belgian ports was made. It was considered likely that the Germans might have attempted to mine the harbour mouth and the nearby channels, but small boats could normally cross minefields safely, and blockships could take their chances with mines as they were expendable.

On this occasion, the objective was to block the harbour mouth by sinking two old cruisers, *Vindictive* and *Sappho*, in the fairway. Their charge into the harbour mouth would be covered by the guns of a monitor and the crews would be taken off by coastal motor boats (CMBs). Four large modern destroyers, *Warwick*, *Whirlwind*, *Velox* and *Trident*, would cover the force against the German destroyers, Keyes hoisting his flag in *Warwick*. It is not relevant here to go into all the details of the action; in summary, the force arrived to find the coast shrouded in a thick fog. *Sappho* broke down and took no part in the action; *Vindictive* blundered about for some time before she found the harbour mouth then successfully sunk herself, but not in a position to block the fairway effectively. The enemy defensive artillery put up a terrific barrage, but the poor visibility made it quite ineffective. *Vindictive*'s crew was taken off in a CMB that had come under fire and was in a sinking condition, but she managed to struggle out as far as *Warwick*. Most of her crew, and the survivors from *Vindictive*, were wounded. Keyes then takes up the story:

By this time the tide had fallen so low that it was inexpedient to return by the route inside the shoals, by which the approach had been made, and I was anxious to get away to seaward as soon as possible, out of range of the enemy's guns before the fog lifted; so a course was steered for a gap in the net defence, by the deep draft route from Ostend, and I withdrew at 25 knots.

It would seem that the enemy had mined the route in anticipation of an attack. At 4 am *Warwick* struck a mine aft and heeled over about 30 degrees to port, and from the bridge it looked as if she was going down stern first with a heavy list; but thanks to the promptness of the Chief Engineer Lieut-Commander R Rampling, who trimmed the ship by adjusting the fuel oil, she righted herself and eventually came to rest on an even keel with the decks almost awash. Fortunately her after engine room bulkhead held until it was shored up, though her back was broken about 70 feet from the stern and the after part of the ship which was wrecked was only held in place by the mine rails (she was fitted for mine laying). The after super imposed gun was thrown into the air and tilted over the side of the superstructure, the men standing by had very narrow escapes. Down below the magazines and store rooms were flooded, and in the wardrooms and cabins the water was almost up to the upper deck in a few minutes. Fortunately no one was in the captain's cabin. Some of the people below had miraculous escapes, including Drummond, who was lying in the wardroom with a smashed thigh. Osborne was there talking to him, and he managed to get him up an ammunition manhole, as they were cut off from the companion hatch. A terrier belonging to the wardroom swam about for a long time before it was rescued...

I gave directions for the *Velox* to be lashed alongside, the *Whirlwind* to take *Warwick* in tow, and the *Trident* to keep a lookout to the eastward to give warning if the enemy destroyers were sighted coming out of Zeebrugge. I gave orders that if they appeared the *Warwick* should be slipped at once, and the other three vessels were to engage them. As Warwick was in considerable danger of sinking all the rescued *Vindictive* crew – except Crutchley, who thought he might be useful to act as First Lieutenant – were transferred to *Velox*. I sent Jackson too to help look after the wounded. He said to me as he left: 'Is this what you call a quiet night? You told me we should be only spectators in the offing.'

Miraculously, the enemy did not intervene and *Warwick* was towed slowly out of danger. The tow was then taken over by salvage tugs from Dover and powerful pumps kept the water in check. The ship was salvaged and went on to serve in the Second World War. She was eventually sunk by a U-boat in the Bristol Channel in 1944. The episode is significant for a number of reasons:

- It shows that ships did not necessarily hit a mine head on. Often, a mine swinging on its mooring would strike alongside or aft.
- It illustrates the rapid flooding and chaos caused by a strike, and the scramble to get onto the upper decks
- It is an excellent example of how quick thinking, in this case by the engineer, could save a seemingly disastrous situation.
- It shows how a determined commander could salvage a ship even if she was disabled in hostile waters.

To return to the events of 1914, the same group of L Class destroyers that had been operating with the unfortunate

Amphion was involved in another incident connected with mining a few weeks later. This time they were accompanied by the light cruiser *Undaunted*. They intercepted a group of four old German destroyers on their way to lay mines in the path of British ships covering the flank of the allied armies in Belgium. The small German ships were no match for this patrol and were all sunk in short order. The action had one most important consequence. A fishing trawler working near the wreck of one of the unfortunate destroyers, *S119*, found a strange, heavy object in her nets. Instead of throwing it back into the sea, the skipper had a look at it and eventually took it ashore and gave it to the local naval depot. It was soon recognized as a treasure beyond price. The package contained the confidential papers of *S119*, which had been thrown over the side in a weighted bag before she sank. Unusually for such a small vessel, *S119* had been carrying the German high-level code books used for diplomatic and inter service communication. With this, the Admiralty intelligence staff could read all the most important German communications, and this was to have an incalculable effect on the outcome of the war. The find was known in Admiralty circles as 'The miraculous draft of fishes'.

The remainder of 1914 saw rigorous and concerted attempts by the Germans to lay effective minefields in the North Sea, where they would do the most damage to shipping. On 26 August the steamer *Albatros*, escorted by a cruiser, stole across the North Sea and laid 194 mines off the mouth of the Tyne, these destroyed a number of neutral ships, but no warships. On the same night *Nautilus*, another converted passenger ship, laid 200 mines off the mouth of the Humber. There was a pause in September, then *Berlin* made her deadly voyage described in the introduction. A yet more daring raid occurred on 3 November, when a force of battle cruisers made their appearance off Yarmouth and started shelling the town and various light forces that happened to be at sea in the vicinity. Not much damage was done, and the big ships soon disappeared into the mists and back to Germany. The raid had had a serious purpose, however. With the battle cruisers had been the light cruiser *Kolberg* with a cargo of 130 mines, which were laid on the fishing grounds of Smith's Knoll. They caused considerable damage to the herring drifters in the area. By some unhappy (for them) chance, the Germans did not escape unscathed. The old heavy cruiser *Yorck* made a navigational error on her return journey and ran onto a German defensive minefield. She was sunk with all but 127 of her 629 man crew lost. On 16 December *Kolberg* was at it again, accompanying a much more serious raid on the north-east coast of England by the German battle cruisers. On this occasion, some extensive damage to life and property was done in Scarborough, Whitby and Hartlepool, and 100 mines were laid in the shipping channel off Scarborough closing the main sea route up the east coast. Although the Admiralty had had some prior knowledge of the raid, the battle squadron sent to intercept the intruders failed to find them, and there was a well justified public outcry at the failure of the Navy to protect the coasts of England. What the public did not know was how bravely and efficiently the minefield was dealt with by the RNMR trawlers from Grimsby with the help of the Royal Navy.

Admiral Charlton had learnt a great deal about mine-sweeping in the first months of the war. The most important element was the tide. German mines were laid moored to their sinker by two cables, the cable reel being mounted inside the sinker (see Figure 4). Their depth was set by hydrostat so as to be a few feet below the water at low tide, making them impossible to see from the surface. If there was a strong tidal stream running they would, of course, be dragged a little deeper by their mooring lines. At high tide the mines would naturally be much deeper in the water – typically 15 feet in the North Sea so they would be too deep to be triggered by a trawler. Charlton forbade sweeping at low tide. It was also found to be too dangerous to sweep in the dark, and this was also to be avoided except in very special circumstances, thus in winter the 'window' suitable for sweeping was very short.

In the two days after the Scarborough raid, several merchantmen were lost in *Kolberg*'s new field, and drifters and other small vessels were deployed to determine, as far as possible, the extent of the minefield. On 19 December, just after dawn, tidal conditions were correct to begin sweeping and the trawlers under command of Lieutenant Godfrey Parsons in the trawler *Passing* steamed north to tackle the mines. It so happened that three fleet minesweepers were in the vicinity commanded by no lesser person than Commander Preston. The events that followed were to cement the bond between the RNMR and the Royal Navy.

It was a brilliantly fine morning with a calm sea, and within a few minutes the Royal Navy sweepers working out to seaward had swept up and detonated two mines; they then turned towards the trawlers in shore. Preston was astonished to hear eighteen massive explosions in less than five minutes as the brave little ships steamed into *Kolberg*'s field, destroying mines as they did so. The tide, however, was now ebbing and mines were bobbing up all round the trawlers. Shots rang out in all directions and from time to time another mine would detonate. Fish stunned by the explosions floated all round. Quite soon, two trawlers were blown up, including *Passing*, which caught fire but was evacuated with only one casualty and eventually towed home. A third, commanded by Lieutenant Crossley RNR, was heavily damaged by nearby explosions, and only saved by Crossley stripping off his clothes and stuffing them into an underwater hole. Preston gave the order to anchor and wait for the high tide. The trawlers and gunboats swung to their anchors as mines floated about around them. When the tide turned the sweep began again but it was not until Christmas that a safe channel had been opened and buoyed. Much of the subsequent sweeping had to be performed in savage winter weather and the conduct of all concerned made a profound impression on Preston. No one panicked. Men rescued from stricken sweepers transferred to others and went on working. Most of all, the skippers and deckhands retained their sense of humour. In all, the minefield accounted for 100 lives lost, fourteen steamers and six minesweepers sunk and a severe delay to coastal traffic.

By this stage in the war it had become clear that the best strategy to deal with German mines was not to try to sweep them all, as a German offensive minefield could equally well serve as a British defensive one, once it was properly charted and buoyed. Rather, it was determined to keep open a swept channel along the east coast, which would be routinely swept daily by trawlers (see Chart 1). The procedure was soon followed in the English Channel and elsewhere. Shipping would be held in a safe area until the daily sweep was completed. Warships would, of course, be protected by the fast fleet sweepers when making aggressive patrols and their probable route would be checked for mines in advance. These routes were known as the 'war channels'. A huge

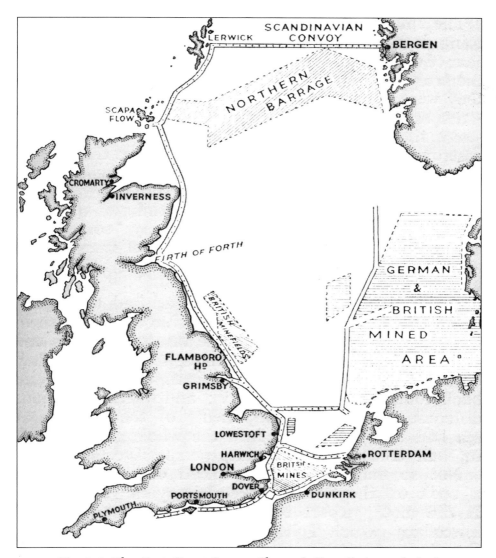

Chart 1: The East Coast Swept Channel. Patrolled regularly by trawlers, this provided a safe route for coastal traffic. The system was extended to cover all coastal passages around the British Isles. Naturally, the German-laid minefields off the British coast were a hazard for German raiders as well as for British commerce.

advantage was gained by the British when they gained access to the German naval codes. There were three levels of code: the highest level code books were recovered as we have seen from *S119*. The level normally used by warships was salved by the Russian Navy from the German light cruiser *Magdeburg*, which went aground in the Baltic. Finally the merchant vessel codes were captured from a liner in Australian waters. Using these codes, together with the direction-finding radio stations that had been established by the Admiralty, it was often possible to anticipate German mine-laying activity and to locate safe channels through their minefields.

The fleet sweepers in use for protecting warships at sea were proving to be hardly fit for purpose. The old gunboats and destroyers used as fleet sweepers were unreliable and had never been intended for extended voyages in the open sea, and the converted ferries were at best a stop gap. An emergency programme was instituted to build a new class of ship, the Flower Class sloops of 1,200 tons. The design was actually based on that of regular whale catchers, which needed to be fast, seaworthy and manoeuvrable. These were to be used for general duties as well as for minesweeping and some of them mounted two formidable 4.7-inch quick-firing guns. They were designed to be as simple as possible to build with a single screw and coal-burning piston engines. Top speed was seventeen knots. The policy worked well, and soon yards up and down the country were turning them out with a lead time of nineteen to twenty-one weeks and no fewer than thirty-seven were delivered in the course of 1915. They proved extremely successful in service, being fine sea boats, and they had excellent survivability when struck by mines or torpedoes. The Admiralty went on ordering them up to 1917 and in the end no fewer than 124 were built. Twenty-eight of them were lost to mines, torpedoes or gunfire. They were excellent sweepers, especially when fitted with new types of sweeping gear that was to emerge later, and they were effective anti-submarine vessels.

For the regular duties of keeping open the swept channels in British waters, a different solution was required. Trawlers were fine sea boats but their deep draft made them seriously vulnerable to the mines they were trying to sweep, and they were too slow to reach newly laid minefields in emergencies. The need to tow mines into shallow water so as to explode them was an additional delaying factor. A faster-moving sweeper would be more likely to sever the mooring cable. Late in 1914 an original solution to this problem had been devised when the Admiralty hired a number of paddle steamers whose peacetime job was to carry passengers for day trips along the coasts – round the Isle of Wight, for example. They had such un-warlike names as *Brighton Queen*, *Westward Ho*, and *Devonia*. These improbable men of war proved to be excellent sweepers; they were very handy, especially if the paddle wheels could be operated independently, as some of them could, quite fast, and they required only a small crew. Their shallow draft of six to seven feet made them able to sweep areas that were far too dangerous for trawlers, and they could haul sweeps at twelve knots, 50 per cent faster than the fishermen, and fast enough to give them a good chance of parting the mooring cables. Very soon, they were to be bearing the brunt of the work of clearing newly laid fields, working alongside the trawlers who kept the war channels open. Like the trawlers, they were manned by their peacetime crews with a sprinkling of Royal Navy personnel. Paddlers had some shortcomings. They were not great seaboats so could not operate in very bad weather and their rudders were insufficient to give the degree of dexterity needed for minesweeping if a big sea was running.

In spite of these drawbacks, so successful were the paddle sweepers that the Admiralty ordered the builder of one of them, Glen Usk, to prepare designs for a new class of naval paddle minesweeper of 810 tons. As these were simple vessels to build and quite small, the building contracts were let to a large assortment of small shipbuilders and engineers, leaving the bigger yards free to build larger warships. Paddle sweepers were fitted with wireless, divided into watertight sections to improve survivability, and carried two 12-pounder guns. Their bows were specially strengthened to withstand harsh treatment and bad weather. Heavy duty winches were fitted to handle sweeping gear. Top speed was fifteen knots. Thirty-two of these ships, known as the Racecourse Class, were built, and they did good service. Ironically, some were sold after the war to become pleasure steamers, perhaps replacing some of the hired paddlers sunk in action. Four of the thirty-two were lost. Some crews argued that the Admiralty paddlers were less good than the best of the commercial ships, as the Admiralty ships had their paddles driven by a single shaft so both rotated at the same speed. Some of the commercial paddlers had independently driven paddles, making them much more manoeuvrable.

Paddlers showed themselves to be tough little ships. In December 1916, *Totnes*, *Cheltenham*, *Pontefract* and *Ludlow* and a few others were sweeping close to Harwich. In command was Lieutenant Bell RN. This was a favourite spot for mines, laid to catch the highly successful and aggressive Harwich

Force of light cruisers and destroyers as they set out into the North Sea. The area was encumbered by wrecks on the sea bottom, which made sweeping very difficult, the sweeps often fouling the wrecks and breaking. Operations had been held up for several days by bad weather, which forced the paddlers to reduce speed so much that the sweeping wires could not be kept off the bottom. Eventually, the weather eased, and they successfully coped with six submarine laid mines, one of which they decided to capture and bring home. They set out in one of the ship's boats, lassoed it with a light line and towed it back to the ship. There it was hoisted up and swung inboard, about two feet above the deck. They managed to remove the detonator, which fell heavily onto the deck, but did no damage. Over the next two weeks about thirty mines were disposed of. On 28 December, more were reported near the Sunk light vessel and two drifters were sent to mark the area, with the sweepers following. Almost immediately, *Eager*, one of the drifters, sighted mines near the surface and made a flag signal, blowing her whistle to attract attention. This was right in the war channel and had to be dealt with at once. Almost as soon as the paddlers got their gear out, *Ludlow* hit a mine and her stern was blown clean off. Thinking that this must have been *Eager*'s mine, *Totness* slipped her sweep and went to *Ludlow*'s assistance. This proved to be a bad mistake. As she turned towards her consort, a mine appeared dead ahead. Putting the engines full astern, the skipper yelled out 'Clear the deck, everybody aft!' sending the crew scampering for shelter. She struck the mine head on. Bell continued his story.

I stepped back behind the standard compass, hunched my shoulders and pulled up the collar of my British Warm [heavy overcoat worn by naval and army officers]. Then the explosion – it seemed to rend the whole ship and shake her to the very core. I fully expected to be hit by falling debris but marvellous to relate, other than a shower bath I was untouched. Afterwards I picked up a bit of twisted iron as big as my fist which must have fallen within a yard of me.

After the explosion I looked over the bridge screen and saw that the entire forecastle up to within twenty feet of the bridge was wrecked. I left the upper bridge and going down met the chief engineer and told him to stop the engines and see if the foremost stokehold bulkhead was tight. I ordered the signalman to tell the *Cheltenham*, our sweeping partner, to take us in tow by the stern, and the *Pontefract* to go to the assistance of *Ludlow* and tow her to Harwich. Groping among the wreckage I came upon one of the stokers, an RNR man, he was in great danger for the deck was cracking ominously and afterwards carried away. I asked him what he was doing and he replied 'I left my jumper here and came to find it. It's got a picture of my young lady in the pocket.'

I went up on deck again and the first lieutenant came up and said 'Shall I lower the boats?' 'What for?' was my reply. 'To abandon ship' said he and then I saw all the boats were manned and ready. I must say I really did enjoy the next few minutes, and my language was hardly parliamentary. Under my abuse the boats became empty and the hands were sent about their work. My steward was running about with the ship's dog in his arms, so I bit into him full and hearty and told him to go and clear up my cabin which, being under the bridge was a mass of broken glass and crockery...

Cheltenham had us in tow stern first in under five minutes, and headed for Harwich. Steering was bad and we yawed considerably. However, we could use our paddles, so continued going slow astern which eased the tow.

Totnes was picked up by a harbour tug and put on a mooring for the night. The damaged bow was cut away and in a few months she was repaired so as to be as good as new. *Cheltenham* helped to tow *Ludlow*, but she foundered in a rising sea that night off the Cork light vessel. The little *Totnes* had survived a head-on mine strike, the mine probably containing 350 lb of explosive. It was thus more than twice as powerful as the one that had done for the mighty *Audacious* two years earlier (160 lb).

Successful as the paddlers were, they had their drawbacks. Apart from their poor heavy-weather performance, the paddle boxes had an alarming habit of trapping mines. Designs were therefore prepared for the Hunt Class twin-screw minesweepers. They were simple vessels, a little smaller than the paddlers, with similar performance and draft. No fewer than eighty-seven of these were laid down, but not all were complete by the end of the war.

One other extraordinary type of minesweeper was employed in the final months of the war. This was the tunnel tug, known as the 'Dance Class'. Tunnel tugs were built for the army for river service in the Middle East. They drew only three and a half feet of water. They were extremely lightly built and slow, and were abominable seaboats; however, being so shallow draft, they were almost invulnerable to mines. They were taken over by the Navy at the end of 1917 and gave good service coastal minesweeping off the French

Chart 2: British, German and American mines laid during the war. The German minefields are in black, whereas the Allied fields are shaded. The underlined figures are numbers of Allied mines, and other figures are numbers of German mines. With their vastly greater resources, the Allies laid far more mines in the latter part of the war, placing them strategically where they would effectively trap the maximum numbers of U-boats. German mines were placed mainly close to headlands where ships would make landfalls and around the approach to major ports. From 1916 onwards, most of the German mines were laid by submarines, whereas the Allies were able to use surface ships, especially fast destroyer-minelayers, to operate close to enemy coasts. The chart gives an idea of how dangerous mine laying and minesweeping operations were as both enemy and friendly mines might be laid in the same areas.

and Belgian coasts and river estuaries. Ten of them were used for this duty.

By the end of 1914, 840 mines had been laid off British coasts, and many hundreds more defensive minefields protected German and Belgian waters from British intruders. Of the mines around the British coasts, some 300 had been swept. (Note: British and German minefields are given in Chart 2.) Some fifty merchantmen had fallen victim to mines. Early in 1915 there was an inconclusive action off the Dogger Bank between British and German battle cruisers, the Germans losing the old battle cruiser *Blücher*. The Germans took the opportunity to lay a large minefield east of the bank to trap British ships chasing the raiders home. This was not very effective, but it interfered with fishing activities in the area. Another large field was laid in April off the Humber, which was extensively used by both naval and civilian traffic. This was rapidly marked and swept, but it caused the loss of twelve ships, including three minesweepers.

Russia was, of course, an important ally in the early part of the war and was practically isolated from the western allies as the Baltic and the Dardanelles were in enemy hands. To complete her isolation, the Germans mined the White Sea, preventing supplies from reaching Russia by the northern route. The Russians had no minesweeping capability and so six Lowestoft trawlers were sent to deal with the menace. This little force was commanded by a retired naval Commander, Leopold Bernays. Bernays was famous for always being in the foremost sweeper and being contemptuous of danger. The little fleet had to cope with large numbers of mines skilfully placed in shipping lanes and around headlands, and with awful weather and lack of supplies. It received precious little help from the Russians, but successfully kept open a safe channel.

The master of a British ship, *Zero*, carrying important Russian officials and £30 million in gold, sent the following report of his experiences in the White Sea.

> … At 11.30 the British sweeper *Bombardier* ordered us to stop instantly. He had four Hull sweepers under his command. Several loud explosions occurred shaking our ship from stem to stern. We anchored and the men in the sweepers, who had not stopped for three days, got some sleep. …at 0.20 am on the 18th we proceeded, in six days they had destroyed over 50 mines. I thought it best to give you this report in detail as I feel the seriousness of the mine danger in the White Sea has not yet reached England and little help can be expected from the Russians.

Later, a similar force was sent to Murmansk.

As 1915 drew on, German surface ships became less active and the frequency of British patrols made conventional offensive mine laying very risky. But another trick was in store.

On 2 July a British coaster, *Cottingham*, ran down a small submarine – *U.C.2* – off Yarmouth. The wreck was in fairly shallow water, about 45 feet, and close to the coast. The master of the *Cottingham* reported the incident immediately and Admiralty trawlers were sent out next day to try to locate the wreck. Dragging the sea bottom with grapnels, they soon found an obstruction, but as they did so they were shaken by a massive under water explosion, which could only have been caused by a mine. Not seriously damaged, they returned to port and soon after a diver was sent down to have a look. It is worth saluting that unknown diver. The water off Yarmouth is murky and the tides run strongly, and he was being lowered in a clumsy diving suit onto a wreck that was liable to explode at any moment. His report was devastating. The tiny submarine had a three foot gash in its pressure hull, which had caused it to flood and sink after striking the coaster, but, most importantly, it was of a hitherto unknown type, and particularly deadly, known as the UC.I. The UC.I class were very small boats, of only just over 160 tons, 111 feet long and with 10 feet beam. They were also slow, with a 90 hp diesel giving 6.2 knots on the surface and electric motors providing 5.2 knots submerged. They must have been a nightmare to navigate in tidal waters off enemy coasts. But their war load was deadly. It consisted of twelve of a special type of mine in six tubes. These were known as the UC mines (see Figure 7). They contained 350 lb of TNT. The mine was designed to sink to the bottom of the sea when released and remain there for half an hour while the submarine got clear. A soluble plug would then dissolve and the mine would find its way towards the surface, unreeling its cable from the sinker as it did so. When a hydrostat in the mine reached the selected depth, it triggered a set of jaws, which clamped the cable, and the mine was ready for duty. The UC.I boats were commenced in 1914, and this boat, *U.C.2*, had been launched only two months before she was lost. Bigger and better mine-laying submarines soon followed, the UC.II class (see Figure 8) of just under 500 tons carried eighteen mines and also had three torpedo tubes. These boats were possibly the most successful submarines built during the war, and were credited with sinking 1,800 Allied and neutral ships. In 1917, they were supplemented by the long-range 1,500-ton UE.II class (see Figure 9), with an improved system of operating

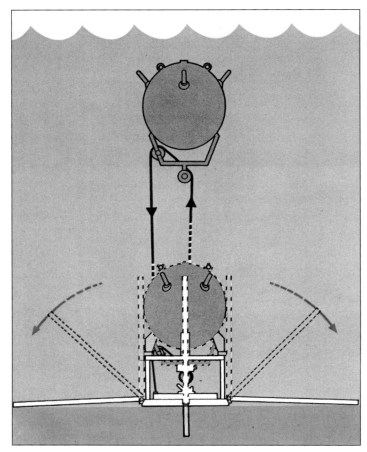

Figure 7: A German submarine-laid mine. The design is similar to the 'egg' mine but it is more compact. When released from the submarine, the mine immediately sinks to the bottom. After a pre-set interval a soluble plug within the base dissolves and the mine is released and floats upward. Four arms are deployed to increase the effectiveness of the mooring. Frequently, the soluble plug was set so as to delay the deployment of the mine for a day or more so that sweepers would think they had cleared a field when actually more mines were waiting on the bottom. In practice there were several cases of U-boats being blown up by their own mines deploying too quickly.

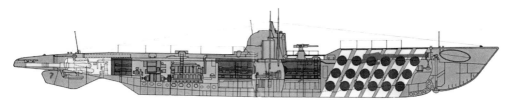

Figure 8: A German UC.II Class U-boat (500 tons submerged). These were the most numerous mine-laying type. The 600 hp engine gave them a surface speed of 12 knots and electric motors provided 7.4 knots submerged. As well as 18 mines, they had three torpedo tubes and a 3.7-inch gun. As the mines were discharged from the forward part on the boat, these subs were in severe danger if the mine was released from its sinker too soon. These boats were extremely effective and played a large part in the effort to paralyze Allied maritime trade in 1916/17.

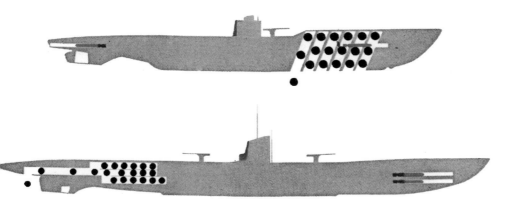

Figure 9: A comparison between the UC.II class and UE.II class. The UE.II class was designed for ocean cruising and had heavier armament, (2 x 5.7-inch guns. 18 torpedoes, 42 mines). Its larger size (almost 2,000 tons submerged) allowed mines to be discharged through the stern. Luckily for the Allies, not many of these boats were completed before the war ended. As it was, they operated very effectively off the east coast of America, sinking the only major US warship lost to enemy action during the war, *Minnesota*.

using horizontal tubes to lay mines from the stern of the boat and formidable gun and torpedo armament.

Submarine-laid mines presented a new and deadly threat. Deposited in small batches in shipping lanes with no warning by a fleet of invisible boats, based in Zeebrugge, close to the vitally important Thames Estuary, they could be fatal to British trade and inhibit movements by naval ships. Losses of Allied ships to mines in the early months of 1915 rose to 103 vessels, including a large hospital ship with a cargo of wounded soldiers from France. Zeebrugge-based boats deposited 648 mines during the year in small fields between Grimsby and the Dover Strait. There was at the time no effective way of locating submarines under water. Hydrophones, which were passive underwater listening devices, could be used but they were ineffective if the boat stayed still under water, and also would not work at all if the hunting vessel was moving or the sea rough. Although submarines were vulnerable to gunfire and to ramming on the surface, they were reasonably safe under water. Their underwater speed and endurance was very limited, but before the days of radar they were difficult to spot on the surface in the dark and so could operate surfaced close to enemy coasts in reasonable safety at night, diving during daytime. Luckily, the UC.I class and the even smaller UB boats were too slow to operate in the strong tides around Dover and the north of Scotland but in the North Sea they now were extremely dangerous. Until the *Cottingham*'s victim was examined, the Admiralty had been reluctant to believe in the existence of submarine minelayers, preferring to believe that the small fields being detected were the work of disguised neutral trawlers. Attempts had been made, fruitlessly, to ban neutral trawlers from British waters and to examine them all closely, but now that the true culprits were identified, action had to be taken.

An effective new weapon was the Actaeon sweep. This was a pair of long wires streamed astern of a sweeper, kept in position by small kites and depth floats so as to stream well clear of the sweeper on each side. As the wire contacted the mooring line of the mine, it slid along it until an explosive grapnel near the kite struck the cable and detonated, severing it, and possibly exploding the mine as well. This was a very useful system as it could be used by a shallow draft sweeper by night as well as by day and would quickly locate any new minefield. As the kite and wire could obviously only be used once, it was not an efficient system to sweep the field, but it did enable a warning Q signal to be issued and the channel closed until properly swept. This type of sweep could also be used as an anti-submarine weapon. It seems that no one much liked using the Actaeon sweep, as dangerous situations could arise if the sweeper had to stop or go astern with wires trailing over the stern and explosive grapnels at the end of them. This nearly caused a nasty accident in Immingham Docks when the sloop *Rosemary* was towed in after being damaged by a mine. She had been using her Actaeon sweep at the time. When moved into the dry dock, it was found that the gates would not close. Underwater inspection revealed that the whole stern of the ship was hanging down underneath her, complete with explosive sweeps. Had they detonated in the dock, the results would have been horrible.

The submarine mine-laying offensive did not immediately mark the end of German surface mine laying. In August 1915 the auxiliary cruiser *Meteor* with a cargo of 380 mines set out from the Jade to lay them in the Moray Firth. This was in response to intelligence which the Germans had received that a large part of the Grand Fleet was in the Firth at the time. *Meteor* had already been active laying mines in the White Sea and was well known to British intelligence. Wireless signals from the Jade were intercepted and de-coded, announcing her departure and Jellicoe was warned to keep a lookout for her off the Norwegian coast, in the expectation that she was again bound for Russian waters. Her appearance off Kinnaird Head was totally unexpected and she laid her mines successfully. On her way home she encountered the armed boarding steamer *Ramsay*, which she sunk in short order before her victim could get a wireless report away. The unfortunate *Ramsay* had taken her for a neutral merchant ship (she was disguised as one) and come alongside ready to board and inspect her cargo. Several prisoners were taken. That evening, however, *Meteor* made a fatal mistake. She sent out a coded wireless message telling U-boats exactly where she had laid her mines and warning them to keep clear. Her wireless operator was clearly not an expert and there were many re-keyings so that there was plenty of time for Room 40 (the Admiralty's intelligence operation) to read the signal and to get radio bearings on the sender. *Meteor*, in spite of her name, was not a fast ship and was intercepted by a force of light cruisers. Having no hope of escape, the *Meteor* scuttled herself and the crew, together with their prisoners, escaped to a neutral fishing boat of which they took control. As one of the light cruisers approached the fishing boat the senior British officer from *Ramsay*, Lieutenant Adkins, managed to signal that there were prisoners on board. 'Steer south west,' was the reply. There was then a brisk argument between Captain Von Knorr of the *Meteor* and Adkins as to which way they should head. Each tried to gain control of the neutral fishing vessel. Eventually, a British fishing boat approached and it was agreed that the erstwhile British prisoners should transfer to that so the affair ended amicably. As the British were departing, Von Knorr became worried that Adkins had been captured in his pyjamas and had no money on him. He insisted on giving him an English £5 note. By some devious diplomatic channel Jellicoe, ever the perfect gentleman, arranged for the £5 to be repatriated to its generous owner in Germany. The minefield accounted for the old destroyer *Lynx* and damaged two sloops, but fast paddle sweepers were sent up from the Clyde to open a channel and then most of the mines were left in place, and indeed the field was extended, to form part of the coastal defence system.

In early January 1916 another daring surface mining operation was undertaken when the raider *Moewe* cruised round the Minch and Cape Wrath laying 252 mines in atrocious weather, frequently passing close to British warships who probably mistook her for one of their own. On 6 Jan the pre-dreadnought battleship *King Edward VII* was steaming from Scapa to Belfast for a refit when she struck a mine – probably one of *Moewe's*. The weather was still rough and towing in the heavy seas proved impossible. The crew were evacuated onto supporting destroyers, which went alongside in spite of the weather, but the old ship sank. She was no great loss, being too slow to operate with the battle fleet at sea. Soon afterwards, this field was located and once again a clear channel was swept, but most of the mines left in place so as to act defensively.

The mine menace was not diminished in 1916, as new UC.II submarine minelayers began to come into service. These were much faster on the surface and under water and as they had a longer range than the UC.I class they could spread their deadly cargo anywhere around the British Isles and the Western Approaches. Although the new sloops and paddlers were now available, there simply were not enough of them to ensure the safety of coastal shipping. There was also the constant danger of the sweepers themselves being attacked by hit and run raids mounted by German destroyers, of which a great many were now based in the southern North Sea. For a time this region became so infested with mines that it was forbidden for warships, except for minesweepers, to operate there.

One important new weapon was added to the defender's armoury – the paravane (see Figure 10). Paravanes resembled an underwater aeroplane, with wings and a fixed rudder and they contained a hydrostat that adjusted the planes, automatically keeping the device a set distance beneath the surface. They were attached to a long wire and streamed from a shoe that was mounted on the bows of the ship, so that the wires, with the paravanes at the end, stretched out at an angle of about fifty degrees to the centre line of the vessel. Except in the unlikely event of the ship striking the mine exactly head on, the paravane wire would deflect it from the ship's side and its mooring cable would slither down the wire to the paravane itself, on which were mounted a pair of steel jaws which cut the cable. This simple device could be used either by sweepers or by other types of warship or merchant vessel to protect themselves. It was not a substitute for the conventional trawler minesweeping operations but it made a great difference to the effectiveness of mines. Initially, paravanes were fitted to warships, but as the war progressed lighter, simpler versions were issued to the majority of merchant vessels.

Hitherto, the German High Seas Fleet had remained pretty well inactive except for the forays of the battle cruisers in the early months of the war, but changes were taking place in Germany and the aggressive and highly competent Admiral Scheer took command of the fleet in January 1916. Immediately, there was more activity and in response the Grand Fleet made a number of sorties attempting to intercept the enemy fleet without result. Each time, Jellicoe was careful to ensure that the fleet sweepers –

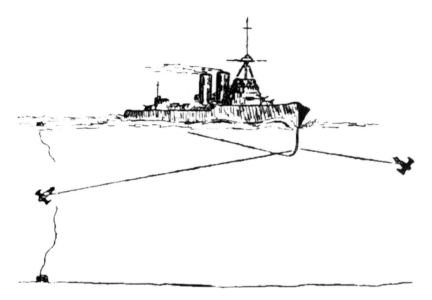

Figure 10: The defensive paravane. The paravane was a most important development in anti-mine warfare. First coming into service in 1916, it was eventually fitted to merchantmen as well as to warships, and was even employed on minesweeping trawlers to give them some protection as they towed their main sweeping gear. They could be deployed by fast ships operating in mine-infested waters near enemy coasts where trawlers could not operate, and by fleet sweepers operating ahead of the battle fleet. Depth of the paravane was controlled by hydrostatically controlled planes and a rudder kept it clear of the ship's side. A cutting jaw severed the mooring cable when it contacted the paravane.

now mostly the new sloops – swept a passage around their bases in case a mine or submarine trap was laid. In May, Scheer's plans for a sortie in strength by the High Seas Fleet, which was to culminate in the Battle of Jutland, began to come to fruition. His strategy was to lure out the British battle cruiser fleet by making an attack with his own battle cruisers on Sunderland, and lead it on to the guns of the High Seas Fleet before Jellicoe with the bulk of the Grand Fleet could come to the rescue. Sunderland was selected as it was thought to be close enough to the battle cruiser anchorage on the Forth to tempt them into a rapid strike against the raiders. The hope was that the Grand Fleet would emerge from this encounter so weakened that the High Seas Fleet could then meet it on equal terms. As part of the same plan, submarines would lay mines in the path of the Grand Fleet and would also be positioned to attack it with torpedoes.

Jellicoe was very conscious that as Churchill put it 'He was the one man who could lose the war in an afternoon.' He was very concerned that in pursuing the Germans he might be led over a minefield laid by the fleeing enemy or into a barrage of torpedoes. He had, as we have seen, made his position very clear in memos to the Admiralty as early as 1914, stating that he would not chase a retreating enemy fleet, and their lordships agreed with this cautious strategy.

Scheer had hoped to make his move to coincide with the Easter Rising in Dublin, but some of his battleships were suffering condenser problems and he could not put to sea. The operation was postponed first until the 17th and then until 23 May. Fifteen U-boats were dispatched to positions off Lowestoft, the Firth of Forth, the Yorkshire coast and the Pentland Firth and duly arrived on station ready to strike at the Grand Fleet and the battle cruisers. But there was another hitch.

Seydlitz, one of the most modern battle cruisers, had taken part in a raid on Lowestoft in March. In the absence of its exceptionally able commander, Hipper, the German battle cruiser force was led by Bodicker, his deputy. This raid had been an attempt to lure the British battle cruiser fleet into a trap by bombarding the English coast, then fleeing eastwards to draw the avenging British battle cruisers into the jaws of the High Seas Fleet, waiting out to sea. Altogether, the raid had been a failure. Reginald Tyrwhitt's indomitable Harwich force put out to meet the heavy German ships. Tyrwhitt turned away to the south when he saw the strength of the German attacking force, perhaps hoping to lure the enemy over the minefields in the approaches to the Thames estuary. The German force refused to be led and bombarded Lowestoft, causing minor damage and killing three civilians. They then turned north and attacked Yarmouth without any result. While they were doing this, Tyrwhitt had turned round and was in action with the escorting German light cruisers and Bodicker turned south again to support his small ships. Soon, the 12-inch guns of the battle cruisers had severely damaged Tyrwhitt's flagship and the Harwich force were hard pressed until Bodicker unaccountably turned away and steamed back to the join the main part of the High Seas Fleet, which was standing by fifty miles to the east. The intended victims of the raid, David Beatty's battle cruiser force, was 200 miles away to the north and took no part in the action.

There had been one serious consequence, however. *Seydlitz*, one of the most formidable of the German battle cruisers, had struck a British mine during the outward journey. This was probably one of the Naval Spherical mines, which normally proved such poor performers but on this occasion it worked well, striking the starboard side of the hull, and tearing a fifty-foot hole in the ship's underwater plating. Eleven men were killed and 1,400 tons of water flooded into the ship. Fortunately, watertight doors prevented the whole hull from flooding so *Seydlitz* was able to limp home and into dry dock. Repairs were expected to take at least two months. When the ship was released from the dockyard, however, it became apparent that the repair was unsatisfactory, and she had to return for further work to be done.

This led to another postponement of the planned operation against Sunderland, and as a result the submarines were near the end of their endurance when the sortie finally took place on 31 May. They had fired torpedoes at some minor targets, all of which missed, and three boats had had to put back into port for various reasons. In the event, none of the others made any notable contribution to the Battle of Jutland. In addition to these, three mine-laying submarines had endeavoured to lay mines in the Firth of Forth, the Moray Firth and off the Orkneys, but had had little success. One returned home with fuel tank trouble, one was sunk by armed trawlers, and one, *U.75*, laid her mines in the wrong place due to a navigational error. Her voyage was not in vain however. The cruiser *Hampshire* struck one of her 'eggs' on 5 June and was lost, together with her distinguished passenger, Lord Kitchener. For the British this was a most unfortunate affair. Kitchener was, rightly or wrongly, regarded as a national hero, and he was travelling to Russia on a military mission. The post-Jutland gale was at its height and Jellicoe had strongly advised him to postpone his journey for a few days, but he had refused and insisted on keeping to his timetable.

Hampshire sailed for Archangel at 4 pm accompanied by four destroyers. She did not take the normal route when leaving the Flow but hugged the coast, hoping to keep out of the worst of the weather. Fearing submarines, the captain called for eighteen knots, but then had to slow down on account of the heavy sea. By 6.30 pm the escorting destroyers were sent home as they could not keep up, and at 7.40 pm, well away from the course normally taken by the battle fleet, she struck one of the mines that *U.75* had mistakenly laid there. It was too rough for boats to be lowered and the loss of life was grave, with only twelve of a complement of over 600 men were saved by drifting ashore on rafts.

To return to the story of the German attempt to use their mine-laying submarines to co-operate with the High Seas Fleet, three short-range UC.I-type minelaying boats had remained in Zebrugge until the High Seas Fleet finally left the Jade. Of these, one UC.1 returned with engine trouble, and the other two successfully deposited their mines in the path of the Harwich force of cruisers and destroyers, but these were swept as a result of the now routine British North Sea sweeping operations before they could do any damage. As so frequently happened during the war, submarines, including minelayers, had been impossible to co-ordinate successfully with the movements of the battle fleet. They were too slow and communications were too difficult.

German mines, in fact, played very little part in the Battle of Jutland. There was no attempt by the retreating High Seas Fleet to deposit mines in the path of their pursuers. German destroyers did have a go at a massed torpedo attack as their fleet fled from the Grand Fleet late in the evening. The torpedoes failed to make any hits, but did halt the British pursuit, saving the High Seas Fleet from a heavy defeat.

Jutland does, however, provide a rare example of tactical offensive mine laying. *Abdiel* was one of the 1,600-ton Marksman class destroyer flotilla leaders. She had a speed of thirty-four knots and was armed with four 4-inch guns, she was thus well able to cope with any German ship fast enough to catch up with her, and could outrun any light cruiser or heavy ship with ease. Instead of torpedoes, which were the main armament of conventional destroyers, she carried up to 100 mines. So successful did she prove, that the Royal Navy converted quite a number of large destroyers into minelayers as the war progressed, and after the war developed a whole class of specialized high-speed minelayers. One of her officers wrote the following account of the action at Jutland.

When the fleets sighted each other and the deployment signal was made the 4th LCS (Light Cruiser Squadron) went off to its station ahead of the line, but *Abdiel* remained where she was until the fleet had nearly finished deploying , by which time 'overs' from the Germans strafing two of our four funnelled cruisers about half a mile to the south west of us and three battle cruisers led by *Invincible* about half a mile to the south east of us, came buzzing about and burst all round us. I therefore legged it round the head of our battle line, which had finished deploying, and managed to get through four lines of destroyers taking up their position ahead of the fleet, and finally got into my battle position half a mile or so on the disengaged side of *Iron Duke* (Jellicoe's flagship). Here we remained until dusk.

At about 9.30 pm I got orders to proceed to a position south of the Vyl lightship and lay a line of mines. [Note: this was in the path of the High Seas Fleet if it should try to flee home via the Horns Reef, down the west coast of Demmark – the course which in the end it actually took.] We therefore went off at 32 knots passing on our way several ships in the distance, which were making a great deal of smoke, but as we were not making any smoke ourselves we presumably were not seen. We reached our position at about 1 am and laid the mines, then we returned to Rosyth for another load, passing south of the big North Sea mined area.

Abdiel was not hit during the battle, and did not have any action with any Hun destroyer or big ships, but we got a very good view of the whole show between 6 and 8 pm. We had 80 ordinary mines and 10 Leon mines on board, all primed, so perhaps it is just as well we were not hit.

The ship did exactly what she was intended to do, justified her existence and that's all there was to it.

Actually, there was more to it. *Ostfriesland*, a German dreadnought, hit one of *Abdiel*'s mines (possibly this one had been laid on an expedition some days earlier), and was heavily damaged. She shipped 400 tons of water and had a hole about forty feet by twelve feet under her forward wing turret. Unlike British battleships, however, she was very well protected, and the torpedo bulkhead held, preventing serious damage to the working parts of the ship. She limped home under escort for repairs, which took two months. The rest of the German fleet sighted mines but kept on going and were lucky not to share *Ostfriesland*'s fate. A buoy dropped by the leading ship to mark the mines was mistaken for a British submarine and subjected to a heavy bombardment.

This was an excellent example of the effectiveness of a fast, well-armed minelayer. It is significant that she was not seen by enemy vessels and this was because she had oil-fired turbine engines, which made far less smoke than coal burners when running hard. Her officers must have been superb navigators, operating as they did at high speed in mine-infested waters, and laying their eggs accurately where they could do the most damage. She continued to operate on high-speed mining missions in waters close to enemy coasts throughout the rest of the war without suffering serious damage. She was probably the most effective minelayer in the Royal Navy.

Apart from operations against the Grand Fleet, German mine laying was halted between May and October 1916 as a result of an American ultimatum demanding a halt to the wanton destruction of merchant shipping. In October, the mine-laying submarines were loosed again and, using the new larger boats, fields were laid as far afield as the south-west of Ireland and the Isle of Man, not to mention over 700 in the entrances to ports and harbours around the English Channel and the east coast. During the year, 1,840 mines were swept but 131 merchant ships were mined and 41 trawlers and fourteen naval vessels of various types shared their fate. Almost 600 vessels, were, by this time, engaged in minesweeping.

1917 was the blackest year for the Allies at sea, with terrible losses being sustained to submarines, forcing the Admiralty to introduce a convoy system, first to the French coal trade, then to shipping to Scandinavia, and eventually to the Atlantic traffic. This at least stabilized the situation as far as submarine attack was concerned, and light began to glimmer at the end of the tunnel during the second half of the year.

U-boats made all-out attempts to catch troopers carrying American soldiers across the Atlantic, but these were normally fast-moving liners, protected by powerful escorts, and not one was lost. It was extremely difficult to intercept a fast-moving escorted ship with a slow-moving submerged U-boat. The American battleship *New York*, however, struck a mine off Liverpool and was damaged. This mine was part of a vigorous submarine offensive mounted off the Mersey, the Clyde and Belfast in 1917, which accounted for ten merchant ships, a destroyer and an unfortunate pilot boat, which went down with the loss of twenty-eight men. A particularly troublesome minefield was established by U-boats off the Maas lightship, right in the path of Holland-bound merchantmen. This was constantly being swept, only to be renewed by submarine a few days later. In all, 680 mines were laid there, of which 635 were swept, at a cost of four merchant ships and eight sweepers.

Although minesweeping and detection methods had improved, the number and range of the mine laying U-boats had, until mid-1917, more than kept up with Allied sweeping efforts, but before the end of the year there were distinct signs of improvement. Some 4,000 mines were swept in 1917, and although probably twice as many were laid as in 1916, shipping losses were only a fraction higher. Losses of sweepers, however, were severe, at one point reaching a rate of one per day. On the positive side for the Allies, thirty-three mine laying U-boats were destroyed, largely thanks to the greater numbers of destroyers and sloops available, some from new builds, some released from the Grand Fleet, and eventually some dispatched from America, including the powerful new flush-decked destroyers. Other U-boats fell victim to the increasingly frequent raids on their lairs in Ostend and Zeebrugge by British monitors. 'War channels' like those established in 1914 along the East Coast were opened up in the Irish Sea, off the west coasts of Ireland and

Scotland and in the western approaches to the English
Channel. To reduce the losses among the sweepers, coastal
motor boats were increasingly used for mine detection and
sweeping, using light sweeps. These boats were so shallow
that they were unlikely to detonate a mine and their mainly
RNVR crews became expert at charting and marking new
small minefields laid by U-boats.

Heavy U-boat losses not only began to exceed German
production capacity, but also robbed her of her most skilled
and determined crews. Air power was also beginning to play
a part. Although it was usually impossible to spot mines
from the air in the murky waters around Britain, aircraft
could locate submarines on the surface, forcing them to dive
and calling up surface vessels by radio. Very extensive air
patrolling of the North Sea, often by obsolete and unarmed

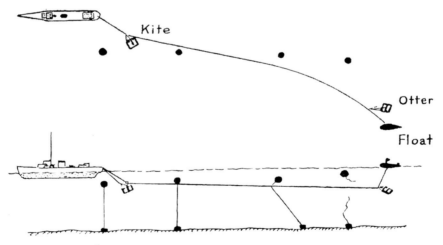

Figure 11: High-speed sweeping carried out by a destroyer. Two
paravanes are used to keep the sweeping wire taut and at the
required depth. This system could be used to clear a wider path for
following warships than the normal paravane system.

aircraft, made the life of U-boat captains increasingly difficult. As we shall see in the following chapters, the effects of British mining and barrages were also of great importance from 1917 onwards. Finally, all merchant ships were, by late 1917, being issued with paravane gear, giving them effective protection from most mines. In 1918, for these reasons, losses to merchant shipping due to mines in British waters were reduced to only twenty-seven ships.

Two significant new sweeping methods were introduced towards the end of the war. The High Speed Sweep (see Figure 11) consisted of a wire with a paravane at each end, towed behind a destroyer by a heavy wire attached to the centre point of the sweep, with a kite at the end of it in order to maintain depth. This enabled destroyers and other light draft vessels to clear a pathway for following heavy ships. The 'Oropesa' sweep (see Figure 12) was designed to be used

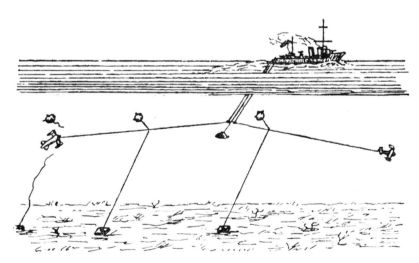

Figure 12: The Oropesa sweep. This was another system used to clear a path for following ships. The ship using it might itself be protected by paravanes.

by formations of conventional minesweepers. It was towed by a single sweeper and consisted of two kites and a float on a long wire. This would be used by the leading ship of a flotilla and would sweep a safe path for the ships behind, which would be working in pairs.

An idea of the work of paddle sweepers at this time can be given by quoting an account of an incident off Dunkirk in June 1917. Dunkirk was close to German bases in Belgium, and was frequently under artillery and air attack, but it was a vital base for the British forces and through it passed most of the food for the Army. The Germans were constantly mining the approaches to the harbour. At dawn, three Admiralty paddlers with Royal Navy crews, *Kempton*, *Redcar* and *Gatwick*, steamed out of Dunkirk to sweep mines reported off Calais. It was a calm day and at first nothing was found. As per standing orders, sweeping was halted two hours before low water, and the three little paddlers anchored in shore. While they were there a hired drifter approached and told them that mines had been seen in the fairway. The story is continued in the words of Lieutenant Thompson DSC, RN.

> We were sweeping three abreast, the area was dotted with wrecks – quite safe for navigation but the devil as far as sweeps were concerned. As soon as we were coupled up the mines began bobbing to the surface. Then *Gatwick*'s sweep parted so I ordered her to sink the three mines that had appeared while *Redcar* and ourselves continued to sweep.
>
> No sooner had the signal been sent when *Redcar* struck a moored mine fair and square under her mess deck. The fore part of the ship was blown away as far as the bridge

and the water was covered with debris and wounded men supporting themselves as best they could. The gun's crew and four other men in the bows were killed instantaneously.

The Admiralty built paddlers were more stoutly built than the ex pleasure steamers, and having ordered his crew to stand by the boat, Lieutenant Daniels, the *Redcar*'s commanding officer, went below with the chief engineer to examine the foremost bulkhead of the boiler room. They found the bottom part of it blown away and water pouring into the hull. It seemed unlikely that what remained of the ship would stay afloat. Her wounded end was nearly under water and her stern lifting. Returning on deck Daniels ordered his crew to abandon ship in boats while he and the chief engineer remained on board to make fast a hawser in case the *Redcar*'s stern portion could be taken in tow and salvaged.

We immediately closed the wreck and sent away all our boats to pick up survivors. Most of the survivors came on board my ship and as there was considerable delay in getting them inboard and I was anxious to get out of the area and to transfer the wounded onto the drifter for passage to Dunkirk, I left the bridge to try to hasten things.

On my way forward I found the chief engineer working over a casualty on the starboard sponson. The poor man had lost one foot and the other was hanging by about an inch of flesh, his abdomen was cut clean open, with the intestines hanging out. We amputated the foot with my sheath knife, put on tourniquets, replaced his inside, and tied him up as best we could. As I began to walk forward a mine hit us in the engine room, just below where we were standing. The chief engineer was telescoped (we picked up his body next day) and the casualty from *Redcar* was blown into the water. Rescued by an Able Seaman called Morrison the poor fellow lived for forty eight hours then died of shock.

One of *Redcar*'s boats had not been made fast onto the *Kempton* when the men were disembarking and drifted some twenty five yards away when the latter blew up. Two of *Redcar*'s men realized there would not be enough room in the remaining boats for the survivors of the two ships. They immediately jumped overboard, swam to the boat and paddled it alongside *Kempton* where it was at once was filled with men. This action saved many lives.

When the explosion came I was thrown about twenty feet and landed in a sitting position on the quarterdeck. I heard no sound but felt exactly as if I had suddenly been placed in a London fog. Both masts had come down and the ship's back was broken. The officer of the watch was blown from the upper bridge to the lower and his trousers were split from clew to earring. I gave the order to abandon ship... The ship was steadily settling amidships with the bow and stern rising out of the water.

As we were drifting towards the barrage I decided to let go the anchor. Just as I was knocking off the slip I remember Richardson remarking 'What happens if we drop the killick [slang for anchor] on another bloody mine?' Luckily we didn't.

By this time everyone was out of the ship except two ABs (I heard afterwards that the first person over the side was my Chow dog Bruin), and as she had taken a heavy list to port Richardson and I went to my cabin to save what we could. On the way I remembered that we still had a destroyer's allowance of confidential books on board, relics of the days when *Kempton* had been sweeping the approaches to the Firth of Forth. So I knotted the neck of a cricket shirt and used it as a sack… We were on our way over to the *Gatwick* when the old *Kempton* turned over and sank, her forefoot remaining above the water for some time. I felt very sad. She was the best built of all the paddle minesweepers and during her year of service had never let me down.

This was just one of many little dramas that took place close to the French and Belgian coasts. The arrival of the tunnel minesweepers and motor boats fitted for mine detection and clearance eventually reduced the casualty rate.

In December 1917 a remarkable series of events took place around a submarine-laid minefield just off the Nab, east of the Isle of Wight. The field was soon discovered by the regular trawler patrol, but in the process the *Apley* struck a mine and sank with loss of life. Further trawlers and paddlers were sent to area, among them *Manx King* under command of a Royal Navy Chief Gunner, Mr Blackmore. The operation took two days, and eventually the area was declared clear and the trawlers were ordered to haul in their sweeps and head for home. As he was doing this, Blackmore was horrified to see that he had hauled up a live mine, wedged in his kite. Not only that, but the mine and the kite were suspended over the stern of his little ship, swinging to and fro in the choppy sea, the mine's mooring tangled hopelessly round the kite. The mine was still attached to its mooring, which was lodged on the sea bottom, anchoring the trawler firmly. One of the horns of the mine were almost in contact with *Manx King*'s gunwale; another was touching the kite itself and was already dented. Blackmore ordered his crew to shut off steam and abandon ship, which they did, and were picked up by boats from the other trawlers. (Remember that this was in the open sea, in December, on a rough day.) Blackmore himself remained on board accompanied by his second in command, Edward Dollin. They determined that if they cut the wire and let the mine and the kite fall into the sea, the mine would almost certainly explode, so they lashed it securely where it was, then climbed out over the stern onto it and removed the horns one by one. They could not get at the safety plug at the bottom of the mine as it was hard against the ship's side. This done, the crew were re-embarked and the mine was disentangled from its mooring. A coastal motor boat was sent to Portsmouth for some special tools and eventually the mine was properly disarmed by the crew, working in the dark, hanging over the stern, in the choppy sea. Blackmore and Dollin were duly decorated and promoted for their valour.

Two extraordinary episodes related to mine-laying submarines in this part of the war are worth relating. One concerns *U.C. 44* a mine-laying U-boat operating off the south coast of Ireland. Over 400 mines were laid there in 1917 and, of these, 330 were swept by an active force of sweepers working out of Queenstown. The sweepers noted that every time they swept a field another would regularly arrive in the same place soon after the sweepers had been at work. The leader of the sweeper flotilla saw this as an opportunity. One day in early August he ordered his sweepers to look busy in the field, but not to deploy their sweeps and to leave the mines in place. This they did. Sure enough, on 4 August *U.C.44* appeared during the night to renew the field, which her Captain believed he had watched being swept. At 22.30 hours the town of Waterford in south-east Ireland was awoken by a shattering explosion as the unfortunate boat

Audacious slowly sinking off Rathlin Island. Destroyers stand by as most of the crew are taken off in the ship's boats. She was the only British dreadnought battleship sunk in the war. Every effort was made to disguise her loss from the Germans as it reduced the Grand Fleet's numerical superiority to only two modern battleships. (*IWM*)

Drifters and trawler in Dover Harbour. These little ships with their fisherman crews bore the brunt of the work to keep the swept channels open throughout the war, working in all weathers, often in difficult and dangerous conditions. By 1918, 412 trawlers and 142 drifters were employed on this work. Many more performed other duties such as net patrol and towage. (*IWM*)

Cavamba working in poor weather in the Bay of Bengal. She was a steamer pressed into service to sweep mines laid opportunistically by German surface raiders such as *Wolf*. (*IWM*)

Princess Margaret was designed as a ferry to work between Seattle and Vancouver, but was rapidly converted into a minelayer and had an eventful and successful wartime career. She could carry up to 500 mines. She was much faster and drew less water than the ancient cruisers that she replaced in the role, and was able to make many daring night time voyages into the German Bight to lay mines. Her high speed enabled her to avoid encounters with enemy warships, which was just as well, as her high, unarmoured sides would have made her very vulnerable to gunfire. (*IWM*)

E.34 in dry dock, showing the saddle tanks that held twenty mines contained in vertical tubes. Two special types of mine were devised for submarine use, both with Hertz horn firing gear. One was a drifting Leon type and the other a moored mine. The E Class were excellent submarines and made good minelayers, although the first, *E.21*, was lost due to an unknown cause in March 1916 on only her second operation. (*IWM*)

Duchess of Rothesay sending a boat to inspect a drifting German mine. She was typical of the paddle steamers, designed to take holidaymakers on pleasure trips, pressed into service as sweepers. They were fast and had a shallow draft, making them ideal for dealing with German offensive minefields laid close to headlands. They were supplemented by the Racecourse class of naval paddlers of very similar design. Their only drawback was their rather poor sea-keeping qualities. (*IWM*)

Mines aboard *Abdiel*. She is carrying a mixture of H.II and Leon mines. Very fast and well armed, *Abdiel* was the first of a family of destroyers converted for mine laying, and was probably the most successful British minelayer ever built. One of her mines severely damaged the battleship *Ostfriesland* in the closing stages of the Battle of Jutland. (*IWM*)

Coastal motor boat fitted for mine laying. These little boats, based in Dunkirk, were used to lay mines off the Belgian coast and in shallow waters of the Thames Estuary and the east coast. These were especially effective in trapping U-boats based in Zeebrugge. They could carry up to three anti-submarine type mines. (*IWM*)

struck one of the mines laid by her predecessor. The captain was rescued, complaining loudly to his captors of the inefficiency of British minesweeping.

Another astonishing series of events was the 'Fred Karno's Navy' attacks mounted on the U-boat bases in Belgium. (Fred Karno's Navy was an appropriate name for the bizarre collection of ships put together for these expeditions.) These were carried out by monitors, shallow-draft ships mounting massive12-inch turrets salvaged from scrapped Majestic class battleships. Undoubtedly the ugliest warships in the fleet, they boasted a top speed of 6.5 knots.

Imagine a fleet of perhaps two dozen ships led by paddle-driven sweepers, designed to take day trippers round some south coast harbour, escorted by thirty-six-knot destroyers and consisting of three or four monitors and a host of drifters and small craft. This unlikely armada would cross to the Belgian coast during a dark night making all of six knots, aiming to arrive off the coast in the dark. Then the monitors would creep close in shore. Small craft cautiously went in even closer and erected tripods on sandbanks, on top of which were perched gunnery observers and signallers. The drifters would lay anti-torpedo nets round the monitors. At dawn a terrific bombardment would open up, with the shot being spotted by observers on the tripods. When the commander, usually Reginald Bacon, the Admiral Commanding the Dover Patrol, considered they had done enough damage, this absurd fleet would make smoke to deter gunners on shore and steam slowly away. At least one mine-laying submarine, *U.C.70*, the boat of the ace Werner Fürbringer, was destroyed by these raids, and many others, together with their supporting shore installations and small craft, were damaged.

Some enterprising German mine-laying expeditions took place during 1917 and 1918. The 6,000-ton steamer *Wolf* put to sea in November 1916 and managed to evade the British blockade. She carried 458 mines and was heavily armed. Her voyage lasted until March 1918, and during it she was able to sow mines off the Cape of Good Hope, Colombo, Aden, Bombay (Mumbai), the China Sea, Australia and New Zealand. Some of the mines were actually laid by a captured merchant ship, *Tirritella*. This bold voyage accounted for about fifteen British and neutral ships. It would have been yet more serious if one of the prisoners taken from a prize ship had not had the bright idea of throwing bottles over the side with notes of where mines had been laid. Two of these were found and this aided the business of clearing up the dangerous fields. So far away from the war there were no minesweepers or sloops so local small tugs, and various locally purchased trawlers, had to be pressed into service. One mine, washed ashore in South Africa, had an interesting fate when a local farmer found it on the beach and decided first to knock the horns off with a hammer, which he did, then he set fire to the contents. These did not actually explode, but sent up a terrific flame terrifying the Boer, his horse, and everyone else for miles around.

When the USA entered the war Germany had some nasty surprises in store. In addition to the formidable UC.II-type minelayers, they had developed a class of long-range 'cruiser submarines', with a range of 10,000 miles at cruising speed. These were known as the UE.II class (see Figure 9). They carried 42 mines and 18 torpedoes. *U-151* had operated off the east coast of the US in May 1918 and did considerable damage, but soon after this *U-117* eclipsed all previous submarines of any nation by her successes, which were unparalleled even in the Second World War.

Departing from Kiel on 11 July, she took a cautious route through the Baltic and the Skaggerak then rounded the Shetlands and made for the east coast of the US with her deadly cargo of mines. Three targets presented themselves as she crossed the Atlantic, two lone steamers and a cruiser, but bad weather intervened and she did not get a chance of a shot at any of them. On 11 August she found herself among a fishing fleet, and sunk nine of the inoffensive American vessels with gunfire and scuttling charges. The next day an armed Norwegian steamer, *Sommerstadt*, fell victim to the first of her torpedoes and soon afterwards an American tanker, *Frederick R. Kellogg*, en route from Mexico to Boston, suffered the same fate. Near the Barnegat Light, *U-117* started her mine-laying operations, which were briefly interrupted first by a passing sailing schooner, which was sunk by gunfire, and then by the intervention of an American seaplane, which ineffectively dropped a stick of bombs. More mines were then laid off the Fenwick Island lightship. Interrupted again by the chance to sink another sailing ship with gunfire, and by another brief encounter with a seaplane, she moved a little further south and completed her mine-laying mission off Cape Hatteras. Now short of fuel she turned for home, sinking five more ships on the way, and making two unsuccessful attacks on well-armed British freighters. She was forced to re-fuel from a U-boat near the Faroe Islands, then managed to make her home port, being towed the last few miles with empty tanks.

U-117's mines had been well placed to trap vessels leaving and approaching the big naval bases at Norfolk and Newport

News and the commercial port at Baltimore. The old battleship *Minnesota* was severely damaged and a naval transport sunk. There were also several merchant ship victims. Altogether, twenty-four American, British and neutral vessels were sunk or severely damaged totalling a little short of 60,000 tons.

On another occasion, in July 1918 *U-156* achieved the distinction of causing the only total loss of a large US Navy ship of the whole war. The victim was *San Diego*, an armoured cruiser built in 1904. She set out from Portsmouth naval yard bound for New York, where she was to pick up a convoy of troopers and escort them across the Atlantic. She was an odd choice for an escort, being an obsolete ship, and although her size (13,900 tons) might have given comfort to the ships of the convoy, she could not have stood up against a German cruiser, and was not handy enough to do much about any attacking submarine. As she passed Fire Island, close to Long Island at a speed of fifteen knots, she was shaken by a terrific explosion. All her gun crews and lookouts were at their stations, and it was at first thought that she had been torpedoed. The crew were ordered to open fire on 'anything that looked like a periscope'. It was not a torpedo that had struck her, however, but a mine recently laid by *U-156*. The strike was on the port side, well below the water line. The explosion had flooded the engine room and caused the ship to heel over to such an angle that water flooded in through the gun ports. Distortion of the engine room bulkheads by the explosion made it impossible to seal off the flooded area effectively. The Captain called for full speed, but the furnaces were soon extinguished and the ship was clearly sinking. As the radio did not work, a boat was dispatched to the mainland to summon rescue vessels. Ten minutes after the explosion the lifeboats were launched, and when he was sure there was no hope, the Captain ordered the men to abandon ship, which they did in an orderly manner, Captain Christy being the last man to leave. Six men were killed, but rescue boats from the shore picked up more than 1,000 survivors from the water. A naval aircraft, sent to search for the offending sub, attacked an underwater target, but this turned out to be the hull of the *San Diego* herself. Later six more mines were found in the area. *U-156*'s luck did not last. She sailed north to destroy a number of small vessels, mostly Grand Banks fishing boats, then she returned across the Atlantic. The crossing was without incident and she and radioed home to say she was about to cross the northern mine barrage. That was the last that was ever heard of her, so it is assumed that she fell victim to a submerged mine.

Germany commissioned eight of these large submarine minelayers during the last few months of the war, and between them they sunk over 100,000 tons of Allied shipping, albeit many of their victims were small fishing boats. They sowed minefields along the east coast of North America from Cape Hatteras up to Newfoundland. Had they all gone into action they might have been a severe menace to the Allies, but naval supplies were so short by that stage of the war, and conditions in Germany so difficult, that the boats undertook very few active service missions.

Apart from these episodes German mine-laying activity began to dwindle in the last year of the war. The large U-boat minelayers now had to contend with formidable difficulties when trying to exit the North Sea and their efforts became concentrated on a few fields near their home ports. One of these was the Maas field, which had given the Allies such problems in 1917. This was now being continuously renewed by two dedicated U-boats and cost the Royal Navy five destroyers. Minesweeping efforts in the area had to be strongly protected because of the closeness to the occupied Belgian coast. Another area on which a lot of effort was expended was the Firth of Forth, outside which U-boats attempted to put down a huge semi-circular minefield. This was extremely unsuccessful because the Germans were so methodical and predictable in their mine laying that the sweepers knew exactly where to look for mines and could deal with them at leisure, unperturbed by enemy interference. Harwich had been plagued by mines throughout the war and this continued during 1918. Some 213 mines were swept there during that year, with the loss of four sweepers.

Besides the U-boats, Germany commissioned two powerful fast surface minelayers. These were built using components that had been made before the war by the Vulcan Yard to fulfil an order for Russia, which was, of course, cancelled when the war broke out. *Bremmer* and *Bremse* mounted 5.9-inch guns and were able to make twenty-eight knots – much faster than a British light cruiser. They were really following the lead set by the British fast minelayers like *Abdiel*, but were much larger and more heavily armed. By the time they came into service the German Navy had suspended most surface operations and they were not much used, luckily for the British, to lay offensive minefields. They did make a successful attack on a lightly escorted Scandinavian convoy, sinking two destroyers and numerous small merchantmen.

By the end of the war the enemy mine-laying offensive had been effectively contained but the cost had been frightening. No fewer than 726 vessels of various types were engaged in mine sweeping and 214 sweepers had been lost. Over 28,000 mines had been swept by Royal Navy and RNMR sweepers. Unlike the Grand Fleet, the minesweeping service had been constantly at sea and in action since August 1914, many of its men being civilians using paddle steamers, trawlers and drifters designed for peaceful purposes. Their bravery, toughness and resolve were in the best tradition of the history of British seafaring.

CHAPTER 4

The Gallipoli Campaign

T he Gallipoli adventure exhibited almost all the characteristics of an ill-conceived military operation. The final objectives were not clear, careful consideration was not given to the resources needed, and there was constant political interference in military and naval operations. Enemy strength and resolve were underestimated and intelligence was poor. It was also a prime example of the phenomenon of 'mission creep'. At sea as well as on land, many brave men paid the price of this bungling.

The campaign is especially important in the story of mine warfare because this was a campaign in which mines so clearly played the decisive role. They were employed with great skill and daring and the British and French inability to counter them was to cost the Allies a bitter defeat.

Turkey had joined the war on the German side partly as a result of the failure of the Royal Navy to intercept the powerful battle cruiser *Goeben* and the light cruiser *Breslau*, which had made a successful dash into the Bosporus in 1914 and were handed over to the Turkish Navy. This was a terrible blow to British prestige and led the Turks to the belief that they had much to gain by siding with the Germans against their traditional enemy, Russia. Britain looked to them like a toothless tiger. It was determined that the Allies should avenge their failure to deal with this situation by forcing a passage through the Turkish-held narrows of the Dardanelles and threatening Constantinople with the guns of their battleships. At the same time, they could destroy the two ex-German warships.

Originally, the plan had been to destroy the forts at the mouth of the Dardanelles with naval gunfire, then the British and French Mediterranean fleets would steam grandly up the Straits, striking terror into the hearts of the Turks as they did so. (A plan of the Straits is shown on Chart 3.) A suitable fleet consisting of British and French battleships attended by destroyers and light cruisers was assembled just outside the Straits, at Mudros. To deal with the expected mine menace there were thirty-five armed trawlers that had made their way out from home waters. At this stage there was no intention to land troops on the Gallopoli peninsula, but a large army contingent was at hand to participate in the eventual conclusion of the mission in Constantinople, whatever and whenever that might be.

A quick look at the chart will show the nature of the task that the Navy was undertaking. The straits are dominated by hilly, broken country and are only about five miles wide at their widest point. The Narrows leading into the Sea of Marmora are less than a mile wide. Ships in the Straits are liable to shelling from the forts at the entrance and from others established at strategic points along the shoreline. The forts themselves were vulnerable structures, but around them had been built, with German advice and help, modern well-protected earthworks concealing heavy guns so that they could survive anything short of a direct hit on the gun itself. In the hillsides looking down on the Straits were

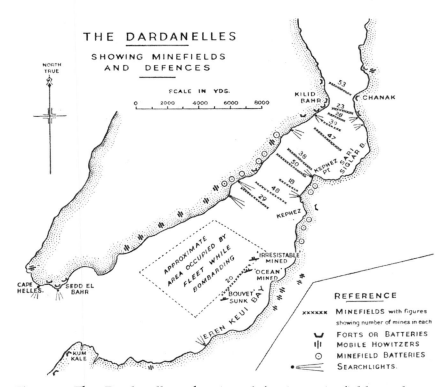

Chart 3: The Dardanelles, showing defensive minefields and fortifications. The forts at Cape Helles and Kum Kale were effectively silenced at least temporally. In approaching close to the forts at Kephez, the bombarding ships ran into the small field laid by *Nousret* in exactly the right place to do maximum damage, inside Eren Keui Bay. In spite of the fearsome minefields in the Narrows, Roger Keyes was convinced that if the battleships had only persisted in their bombardment and the sweepers had done their job properly, the passage could have been forced. Had paravanes been available and fitted to all the warships involved, their task would certainly have been easier. Unfortunately, these did not come into service until 1916. It is easy to sympathize with the trawler crews who refused to battle against the strong current in the Narrows so close to enemy gun positions and searchlights. They were especially vulnerable when they stopped to get in their sweeps and turn around before returning downstream.

concealed mobile batteries of field guns and howitzers. These were not big enough to damage heavily armoured ships much, but they could be fatal to unarmoured vessels such as trawlers or destroyers. There were also powerful mobile searchlights to spot for the guns at night. Through the Straits runs a current of anything from two to four knots, constantly running out into the Mediterranean. This current runs strongly in the centre, but is weak or non-existent near the shores, especially the southern (Asiatic) shore. There could scarcely be a more suitable stretch of water for defensive mining.

Turkish forces were stiffened by a German contingent mostly made up of specialist troops and artillery men commanded by the highly competent General von Sanders. Supplies of ammunition and armaments constantly arrived by rail from Germany.

The Turks had plenty of experience of mines, gained in their wars with Russia, and in this area also they received invaluable technical help from Germany. They had a brilliant naval mine expert, Lieutenant Colonel Geehl. Three sorts of mine were available to them. Firstly, they had floating mines, which were attached to small rafts and could be floated down on an enemy at the mouth of the straits, driven by the current. These were employed on at least one occasion but were not effective. Secondly, there were Leon-type mines. These, as we have seen, were another type of free floating mine, which had an electric motor and propeller controlled by a hydrostatic valve to keep them at a constant depth. Leons had the advantage of being difficult to see from the surface and they could be used in water too deep to moor conventional mines. They were also almost impossible to sweep as they had no mooring cable. The Turks did not, in the end, employ their stock of Leons, but they might have done so if the invaders had penetrated into the deep waters of the Sea of Marmora. Thirdly, they had conventional Hertz horn mines, able to be laid by fast civilian steamers, destroyers or torpedo boats. All the Turkish mines were imported, mostly from Germany.

The Narrows of the Dardanelles had been mined before the war, in mid-1914, but merchant ships were allowed to pass through a clear channel, accompanied by a pilot. In September of that year, however, a British patrol intercepted a Turkish destroyer just outside the Narrows and found German sailors on board. The resulting diplomatic incident caused the Turks to close the gap in the minefields and declare the Narrows closed. On 31 October Turkey joined the war on the German side. Immediately, the minefields were reinforced, and the shore-based heavy artillery and mobile field guns were increased in number. Their crews were rapidly stiffened by the German artillery specialists. More powerful searchlights were sent to cover the minefields and keep away sweepers. The old battleship *Messudieh* was sent into the Narrows to provide extra protection and fire power. Vice Admiral Sir Sackville Carden, who commanded the British and French ships off the Dardanelles, made two attempts to destroy forts guarding the entrance, doing considerable damage, but failing to silence them completely. The protective earthworks, reinforced with German help, ensured that although the guns might be dismounted and the gunners evacuated during a daylight bombardment, it was a relatively simple matter to restore them during the hours of darkness. Only a direct hit on the gun itself would effectively destroy it. The only notable Allied success was the sinking of *Messudieh* by the submarine *B.11*, which managed to dive below the mines and stem the current in the Narrows, although her underwater speed was only four knots.

By the end of January 1915, the War Cabinet had determined to adopt a more aggressive policy with the hope of forcing Turkey out of the war altogether. A fleet ten British and four French old pre-dreadnought battleships would force the Narrows and steam towards Constantinople, protected by minesweepers and destroyers. The entrance forts would be silenced by their guns, supported by the great 15-inch guns of *Queen Elizabeth*, the Navy's most modern and formidable battleship. She was not allowed to penetrate the Straits themselves – that would be too risky – but she could bombard from far off. Unfortunately, accurate long-range indirect gunfire was impossible without good spotting from the air, and this, for various reasons, was not available. Carden had proposed this scheme and it was endorsed by the War Cabinet in the face of opposition from Fisher, the First Sea Lord, who correctly foresaw the danger from mines and the problems associated with attacking coastal artillery from the sea. He also preferred his own competing and equally risky strategy of attacking the German Baltic coast, again using obsolete battleships destined for the scrap yards. He was overruled by the First Lord of the Admiralty, Churchill, and by the practically universal opinion of the Cabinet.

The attacks on the forts commenced on 19 February, and by the 25th most of the guns in the outer forts had been destroyed by the ship's bombardment and by Royal Marine landing parties. The fleets were now able to move into the mouth of the Straits and silence the inner forts guarding the entrance to the Narrows. This was less successful, and once again the gunners took cover when they were being hit by naval gunfire, only to emerge as soon as it ceased. Furthermore, as the ships entered the restricted waters, they came within range of the mobile field guns. These could not do severe damage to heavy ships but they did make matters extremely difficult for the intruders, and forced the destroyers to keep moving so as to avoid being hit. Firing on the inner forts at long range did little damage to them and it was clear that the warships would have to get closer for their assault to be effective.

The first section of the Strait was clear of mines, but to move further in and tackle the second pair of forts at the entrance to the Narrows themselves at close range, the minefields would have to be swept. To do this, the North Sea trawlers had been provided, and these were given light armour to protect them from small arms fire. They were manned by their regular RNMR crews. It had originally been intended to supplement these with 'mine bumpers'– cargo ships with reinforced hulls filled with concrete, which would clear a path for each capital ship by steaming through the field blowing up mines as they went. These were not eventually provided. (Strangely, the British did not make much use of reinforced mine bumpers to protect capital ships in either world war. The Germans used them, calling them *Sperrbrechers*). The trawlers had to battle against the strong currents in the Straits, so that their speed over the land was only two or three knots, making them easy targets for guns on shore. To give them some protection from shore batteries the sweepers were detailed to work at night and were supported by destroyers and a light cruiser. On 1 March they set off on their first mission. Before they reached the minefield they were detected from the shore, and illuminated by brilliant searchlights, making them an excellent target for the shore-based field guns. No trawlers were hit, but the fisherman crews hastily withdrew. They had not been trained for work under fire and were badly shaken by the experience.

Who can blame them? Their little ships were almost stationary in the strong current, and a single hit from the 4-inch or 6-inch field guns would have proved fatal. Three more attempts were made, the last one with battleship support to try to silence the coastal guns, but with no result. A different tactic was then tried. This time the trawlers steamed upstream as fast as they could go, with their sweeping gear stowed, then turned and deployed their kites, letting the current carry them back with engines going slow ahead. A handful of mines was recovered, but some of the crews were so scared, especially when they had to turn round and deploy their sweeps under fire, that they did not attempt to sweep at all. After two weeks of failure the regular Navy was becoming disillusioned with the fishermen-sweepers. One trawler had been sunk and several damaged, but no one had been killed and there were open accusations of cowardice levelled at the RNMR. On 13 March one final attempt was made with the sweeper crews stiffened with Royal Navy volunteers and supported again by fire from a battleship. This was even more disastrous. The supporting cruiser, *Amethyst*, was badly hit, suffering twenty-four men killed, and several trawlers were badly damaged, also suffering casualties. A few mines were swept, and some more were found floating free in the Straits. Possibly, these had been deliberately floated down by the Turks. They were easily dealt with and in future operations small picket boats operated alongside major ships to deal with any more 'floaters'. This was a pretty high-risk operation for the picket boat's crews, exposed as they were to the fire of field guns on shore. Some of them were actually fitted with explosive sweeping wires and seem to have accounted for several mines.

By this point Carden was coming under severe pressure from Churchill who urged him to make progress regardless of casualties. After all, he argued, thousands were dying on the Western Front and the Dardanelles operation could relieve pressure on the hard-pressed troops in France. It was well worth hundreds of casualties among the minesweepers to force the passage and achieve their objective. The minesweeper crews did not agree.

The unfortunate Carden fell sick and was replaced by Admiral de Robeck, who had been his second in command. He resolved to continue with a new tactic devised by Carden of making a daylight attack on the shore batteries and to sweep the minefields as he went. He intended to use his full force now, consisting of thirteen British and four French battleships, and one dreadnought battle cruiser. The battleships were all pre-dreadnoughts except for the super dreadnought *Queen Elizabeth*. A heavy bombardment at long range would attempt to silence the shore batteries and suppress the guns in the forts, then a second wave of battleships would steam close to the forts and complete their destruction, covering the passage of trawlers into the minefields. The warships could then follow the sweepers and force their way right through the Narrows. Some of the attendant destroyers were adapted to carry light sweeping gear.

The action opened as planned. Turkish shore batteries replied vigorously, but the only ship badly damaged was the French *Gaulois*, which had to be beached. Gradually, the warships got the better of the shore guns, and things were going according to plan when the advancing second line of battleships, steaming close to the forts to blast them at close range, suffered a series of appalling disasters. *Bouvet* (French) and *Irresistible* (British) were sunk by mines where there should have been none, and the battle cruiser *Inflexible* was severely damaged by gunfire. Shortly afterwards, the battleship *Ocean* was disabled by gunfire and a mine strike and had to be abandoned. Once again, to the disgust of the naval officers present, the trawlers fled from the scene under heavy bombardment. Two of them had tried to deploy their sweeps and steam upstream. They dealt with three moored mines, but fire from the shore was too much for them and they abandoned their attempt in spite of orders shouted from the picket boats and destroyers. It was impossible now for the battleships to proceed into the Narrows and de Robeck had no alternative to withdrawing his battered force. What had happened was that Lieutenant Colonel Geehl had anticipated a close-range attack on the inner forts and had taken a small fast steamer *Nousret* down the Narrows and laid a small field of twenty Hertz-type mines in exactly the right position. Hence, an insignificant little civilian craft had brought about the sinking of three major warships and the disablement of a dreadnought battle cruiser.

Roger Keyes, the fire-breathing chief of staff, took a destroyer into the Straits that night to look for survivors and to see that *Irresistible* was sunk and could not fall into enemy hands. He reached the conclusion that the Turkish guns had been completely overwhelmed and if only the mines could be cleared the job was almost done. It could be finished off, he thought, if only the minesweepers were manned by volunteers from the stricken British ships and the civilian crews sent home. This was at once set in hand, although a few fishermen elected to remain with their boats. The losses, however, had severely shaken de Robeck. He would not authorize another attempt to force the Narrows until the land on the European shore was in the hands of the Allies. Then the mines could be swept and the forts overwhelmed without interference from field guns and searchlights. Thus began the terrible story of the Allied Gallipoli land campaign. Keyes was appalled. He remained convinced that with properly crewed and supported minesweepers the Navy could have delivered a significant victory. He complained for the rest of his life that it was the over-cautious attitude of his superiors that had deprived the Royal Navy of success. Nor was he a man to give up easily. As the decision to withdraw the unsuccessful expeditionary force was being taken, in November 1915, he argued strongly for a final attempt to force the Narrows with a force of old battleships fitted with makeshift sweeps, escorted by a fleet of navy manned minesweepers and by destroyers fitted with minesweeping gear. He was overruled. Even as late as the winter of 1917/18 he was convinced that he could lead a force of destroyers fitted with the new paravane minesweeping gear up the Narrows and force Turkey, Bulgaria and Romania out of the war. He extracted a promise that he should lead such an expedition if it was ever mounted, although by that time he was, as we shall see, deeply involved in even more important activities. The episode remains a significant defeat for the Royal Navy and an example of how not to plan a campaign.

Naval warships did successfully make their way through the Narrows and up to Constantinople, but they were submarines, which could dive under the mines. They operated extremely effectively for a time in hostile waters. They were fitted with tubular steel fenders around their hydroplanes to prevent them from getting entangled in mine moorings; nevertheless their crews had to endure the terrifying sound of the cables grating on the hulls as they forged slowly up against the current. On one occasion *E.11*, captained by the famous Martin Nasmith, actually got entangled in a mooring cable when returning down current towards home. The mine wobbled about just clear of the hull, making the submarine very difficult to handle as she towed mine, cable and mooring towards the open sea. One touch of the horns would have spelt disaster. Only the Captain in the conning tower could see the mine and he wisely kept his cool and did not inform his crew of their terrible predicament until it was over. He kept the boat going until he reached clear water, then went full astern. To his immense relief, the mine drifted free.

The poor performance of the minesweeping trawlers in this campaign is in stark contrast to their exploits in the North Sea. On many occasions in home waters they performed brilliantly under fire from shore batteries and from ships and submarines, their crews oblivious to the dangers facing them and frequently astonishing their Royal Navy colleagues by their fearless conduct in minefields and under attack. But something in the Dardanelles campaign clearly fazed them. Perhaps it was the unfamiliarity of the location and the local weather. Perhaps it was the terrifying experience of being picked out and followed by powerful searchlights. Maybe the strong current and their very low speed over the ground upset them. Even accounting for these factors, it is difficult not to conclude that there was somewhere a lack of leadership by the regular naval officers present. Keyes's account of the campaign makes it clear that he and his colleagues became furious with the trawlermen and accused them openly of cowardice. He contrasts their conduct to that of the naval crews of the launches, mostly commanded by young midshipmen, which searched fearlessly under fire for floating mines. But you do not get the best out of a tough North Sea fisherman by calling him a coward. Ultimately, of course, the blame must fall on the Admiralty and its planning of the campaign. It was quite wrong to rely on amateurs and civilians to undertake the vital task of minesweeping under fire. They had not been recruited for this and should never have been asked to do it. Their little ships were unsuitable and they were not trained for this sort of arduous service. It was well known that mines were going to be the main problem facing the capital ships and the battleships should have been accompanied by fast fleet minesweepers able to sweep rapidly against the current and manned by naval personnel. This was, after all, the invariable practice of the Grand Fleet when it went to sea. Altogether, it was an example of the poor planning and staff work, which was typical of the campaign. A joke used to circulate in the trenches on the peninsula. A Turkish soldier was paid a bounty of five shillings for each enemy soldier shot, a pound for a junior regimental officer, and five pounds for a senior officer. If he shot an officer on the planning staff, however, he was fined ten pounds.

Ironically, the German battle cruiser *Goeben*, which had played a large part in persuading Turkey to enter the war on the German side, herself was disabled by British mines in 1918 when she eventually steamed out into the Mediterranean.

After their RNMR seamen went home, the trawlers remained busily engaged with their volunteer Royal Navy crews, acting as dispatch boats for the fleet of warships and transports engaged in the Gallipoli landings. They also had to keep an eye out for stealthy Turkish night-time mine laying. This work gave many junior officers their first command. In this role the trawlers were worked very hard, and the young officers were glad of a chance to show their mettle. They were amused to find that the compasses on the trawlers were wildly inaccurate, which led to some exciting night-time voyages. One trawler managed to take thirty-six hours to make the forty-mile leg from Tenedos to Mudros, spending most of the time following its compass course, which took it round and round in circles. There were competitions to see how many soldiers, fully armed and equipped, could be crammed onto a trawler. One young skipper boasted embarking 535. They towed boatloads of troops and stores ashore under heavy fire, laid moorings and carried messages. They proved so useful that more trawlers were sent out from England, complete with their regular fisherman crews. One of these was hit in the funnel by a shell that didn't explode, and the skipper wanted to leave it there as it was too much trouble to take it out! To his fury the Navy decreed that it was too dangerous for nearby ships to have a trawler with an explosive funnel working among them.

Gallipoli provides a classic case of a successful defensive mining operation, carried out with minuscule resources by a relatively weak power and at minimal cost. It also showed the great advantage to be gained from covering a minefield by fire so that it was dangerous to sweep, and ships entering it would be faced by two threats at the same time. The campaign also showed how mines enabled a weaker power to defy a far superior navy. The later stages of the war were to demonstrate an entirely different aspect of mine warfare, in which mines became the preferred weapon of the stronger power.

CHAPTER 5

The British Mine-laying Offensive

The Victorian Royal Navy, as we have seen, never had much time for sea mines. Indeed, a strenuous effort was made to get then banned altogether at The Hague Conference in 1907. They were regarded as sneaky weapons, unable to distinguish between combatants and neutrals, and resented because they seemed to favour weaker powers thus denying Great Britain the fruits of her overwhelming maritime superiority. The Admiralty seems to have lived in the hope that The Hague convention rules would prevent extensive mine laying by the enemy. The Royal Navy disliked the idea of laying mines itself because of the danger to merchant shipping and the fact that minefields would restrict the Grand Fleet and the Channel Fleet manoeuvres. Interestingly, the Germans had had much the same debate about mine laying in the Heligoland Bight. Before the Battle of the Bight, in which the Royal Navy, in spite of shambolic planning and staff work, was able to inflict a severe defeat on German light forces in the Bight, Germany had resisted the temptation to lay minefields close to its coasts except to protect fleet anchorages. If mines were laid, it was argued, the High Seas Fleet would not be able to come out and cut off marauding enemy warships. The Battle of the Bight caused so much angst that the objections were abandoned. In the event, as we shall see, the enthusiasm for mine laying on both sides developed an inverse relationship to the perceived likelihood of a clash between the rival fleets. As British hopes of a 'second Trafalgar' in the North Sea waned, so interest in the potential of offensive mining operations increased.

Mine development was the responsibility of HMS *Vernon*, the naval torpedo and electrical development establishment at Portsmouth, and there was no shortage of excellent ideas, but the will and the funds to develop them were almost entirely absent. When war broke out in 1914, British mine-laying capability was remarkably weak. Some observation mines controlled from the shore had been brought out of retirement and were installed so as to protect important fleet anchorages. The British stock of moored mines was pathetically small in comparison to that of the Germans, consisting of about 4,000 mines, mostly of the naval spherical type, fired by means of a firing arm and striker. They were moored by a single cable 50 fathoms long. Depth setting was reasonably accurate, but the mines themselves were extremely inefficient, often failing to explode when struck, and continually dragging their moorings if laid in a tideway. There was also a handful of the British 'Elia' type mine. Elias were a modified version of an Italian design, not unlike the naval spherical type, but with a more effective firing mechanism. Various other designs had been tried but rejected, often for cost reasons. There was no official strategy for mine laying, and the only mine laying ships in the Royal Navy were a handful of converted obsolete cruisers.

At the Admiralty, mine-laying operations were directly

controlled by Vice Admiral Sir Henry Oliver, the Chief of Staff between October 1914 and November 1917. With conflicting views about the best use of mines prevailing at all levels of the service, it was difficult for him, in the early years of the war, to develop an effective policy. Oliver was also acutely conscious of the difficulty in laying mines accurately, and of the danger to our own submarines and minelayers of mines laid, or turning up in, the wrong place. He might well have added that the tendency of British mines to drag their moorings meant that they were a hazard to everyone, wherever they were laid. The situation was not improved by Fisher as First Sea Lord, who at times proposed grand plans for mining close to German harbours, then reversed his policy a few months later.

The Admiralty was made aware of the poor quality of the British mines, and Fisher established a 'Committee to Enquire into the Present Mining Service' under the direction of Vice Admiral Sir Robert Ommanney. Fisher had a high regard for Ommanney, but his confidence was misplaced and the committee's bungling led to unnecessary delay in producing effective mines. Even as late as June 1915, Ommanney severely criticized the newly appointed commander of the Mine Laying Squadron, Captain Frederick Litchfield-Speer, for expressing his doubts about the effectiveness of British mines, refusing to acknowledge their many faults. At this very time a German U-boat commander was boasting (accurately or not, it is not clear) that he had made a long passage with two British mines draped around the conning tower of his boat. Fisher, however, always the innovator, remained convinced that mines had an important part to play in sea warfare and kept pressure on for development of a coherent aggressive mine-laying strategy, but never seemed to have a consistent view as to where to apply it. Churchill, on the other hand, was so taken up with various aggressive schemes for use of the Royal Navy that he gave little time or thought to the subject.

As early as September 1914, in fact, the appearance of U-boats in the Channel and the aggressive German mine-laying offensive resulted in pressure being brought to bear on the Admiralty to protect the cross-Channel routes with mines. As ever, there was strong resistance to such a tactic on the grounds that it would be a danger to vital coastal navigation and would inhibit the operations of the fleet. These were eventually overruled and on 3 October the old cruisers *Intrepid*, *Iphigenia*, *Andromache* and *Apollo* set out to lay mines off Ostend and to the north-east of the Goodwin Sands. They were not laid in the Dover Strait itself, as the strong tidal stream made mine lying impossible with the equipment then available. As demanded by treaty, an official notice to mariners was published to warn neutrals and merchant ships of the danger. All went according to plan except that immediately the mines had been laid it was determined that troop reinforcements should be sent to Belgium via Zeebrugge. However, the route was now blocked by the new British minefield. Sheepishly, the Royal Navy had to set about sweeping the field it had just laid. The deteriorating military situation on land and the loss to the Allies of most of Belgium resulted in these fields being re-laid by French minelayers a few weeks later. The French mines were of the Breguet type, which was triggered by water pressure acting on a trigger which in turn released a firing pin.

Belatedly, the Navy started to search for new sources of mines and expertise. Some Russian mines with Hertz horns were delivered to Britain and used to defend fleet anchorages. A small number of 'creeping' mines with moorings designed to allow them to move, driven by the constant in shore currents along the north German and Danish coasts were put down on an experimental basis, but this practice was soon abandoned when it was realized that these constituted a danger to our own submarines.

This hesitant beginning did not conclude mine-laying efforts in the first months of the war. Protective fields were laid off Lowestoft and close to headlands that the navy expected U-boats to use as navigational marks when approaching the British coast. In these days of electronic and satellite based navigation systems, it is often easy to forget the difficulties of navigation in the early twentieth century, especially in small vessels moving slowly in tidal waters and guided only by a compass, a lead line and a distance log. The only way to fix position accurately was by taking visual bearings on recognized features on shore. Submarines would therefore be forced to surface so as to fix their position accurately by taking bearings on features on shore. Years of experience taught the Royal Navy where this was likely to happen. At the same time a large number of new mines were ordered. These were mostly the normal spherical type, but there were also some more of the British Elia mines. For some reason the Admiralty still had great confidence in the Elia mine, although in reality it was not much better than the conventional spherical and showed an even more alarming tendency to drag its moorings. Several laid in the southern North Sea finished up almost twenty miles from where they were moored. They also had poor accuracy of depth finding.

As the winter wore on, mining to the east of the Dover Strait continued with no fewer than 7,000 mines being laid to trap ships attempting to interfere with cross Channel traffic. These were not very effective as so many of the mines either sunk or drifted off station. An attempt was also made to lay heavy nets from Folkestone to Griz Nez, but the tidal streams were too strong and the effort was abandoned until the submarine crisis in 1917/18 when, as we shall see, a far more substantial barrage was commenced.

Early in November the Admiralty issued a notice to mariners stating that as the Germans were mining indiscriminately they had no alternative but to reply in kind, and the whole of the North Sea might be subject to mining. Any neutral or merchant ship approaching the North Sea from the north did so at her own peril. Ships were advised to approach via the Dover Strait, from where they would be given directions for a safe passage to neutral ports. This system was maintained throughout the war. There was a lively debate about the advantages of mining the Heligoland Bight, so as restrict the operations of the German High Seas Fleet and U-boats. To do this there was an urgent requirement for more and faster minelayers. These had to be fast ships that could dart into the Bight in darkness, lay their eggs, and return to safety before being detected. The old cruisers, which were the only ships fitted for mine laying, were inadequate for the task as they could only make fifteen knots at best, were twenty-five years old, had obsolete 4.7-inch guns, and were frequently unreliable. The following merchant ships were initially requisitioned for the purpose:

- *Angora:* A 4,300-ton ship, in the event too slow for most mine-laying operations. She carried 300 mines.
- *Biarritz:* A 2,700-ton ship, able to make 21 knots and very useful for short-range operations.

- *Orvieto:* A 12,000–ton ship, carrying 600 ready-to-use mines and a further 600 in the hold. Like *Angora*, she was too slow to dash into the Bight safely and drew too much water. She was eventually released back to her owners.
- *Paris:* A 2,000-ton ferry able to make 21 knots, ideal for short-range mine laying.
- *Princess Margaret and Princess Irene:* These were two new ferries designed to run between Vancouver and Seattle. These were good, fast ships (21 knots) of 5,500 tons, with light draft, and could carry 500 mines. Unfortunately, *Princess Irene* blew up at Sheerness while preparing mines for laying and was lost with all hands. This was a serious blow to the mine-laying campaign. The accident was probably due to the malfunctioning of a firing pistol of an obsolete type.

This heterogeneous fleet was inadequate even for the limited extent of mining proposed early in the war, and it was constantly increased as more ambitious mine offensives were proposed, these developments culminating, as we shall see, in a new class of fast, specially designed, mine-laying warship. Various other merchant ships were pressed into this service in British waters and in the Mediterranean as the war progressed, and eventually even one old battleship (*London*) was employed.

Before these new vessels were brought into service the first field was laid in the Bight by the old cruisers, at considerable risk to themselves. They were subsequently all paid off, except for *Iphigenia*, which was retained in service in various roles, finally ending her days as a block ship used on the Zeebrugge Raid. The crews of the other cruisers were made available for work on more modern ships. The new ships were quickly brought into service and some further offensive mining operations were carried out in the later part of the year.

A German Hertz type mine was recovered intact early in 1915 and as the inadequate performance of the Naval Spherical mine was already apparent some of the German design features were soon adopted. The recovery of one of the first German mines intact is a story in itself. Lieutenant Parsons, a distinguished minesweeping officer, was ordered to retrieve a mine washed up on a beach, make it safe and bring it into port on his trawler. There was no way of knowing if it had been rendered safe by breaking free of its mooring, but following orders Parsons went ahead with his ticklish mission. His first thought was 'What the blazes am I supposed to do.' The little bay where the mine was stuck was bounded by some very dangerous rocks and above it was a 200 foot cliff. How was he supposed to get near the thing, and how on earth could he get his ship close enough to take it on board? He went ashore and contacted the local Territorial Army HQ, and with a detachment of 'Terriers' and a large part of the local population come to see the fun and (with luck) hear the bang, marched to the top of the cliff. Parsons was lowered down the cliff by a rope, and got to work on the mine, being careful not to touch the firing horns. He successfully removed the fuse and gave the signal to the troops above to haul him up. This they willingly did, but their enthusiasm was almost fatal. The rope got caught round the unfortunate Lieutenant's feet and he came up upside down and unconscious. As if this wasn't enough, the rope parted just as he reached the top, and he fell some distance before a safety rope, which he had wisely rigged, broke his fall. Once he had regained his senses, he managed to get the local Rocket Brigade, a part of the civilian lifesaving service, to help him put a line around the mine and fire the other end of it far out to sea. There it was picked up by the trawler, the mine was hauled in and hoisted on board. Parsons was amused to see members of his crew hitting the horns with a hammer 'just to see if I had done my job properly'.

At roughly the same time the activities of the German mine-laying U-boats became known. The recovery of the first submarine-laid mine gave rise to another story of conspicuous gallantry. The mine was spotted near Cape Wrath. An armed yacht managed to get a line attached to its mooring and towed it near to the shore, where it was beached close to some houses. What to do next? The mine was high and dry at low tide but its detonator was stuck in the sand. If it was rolled over the horns of the mine would be fractured and it would explode. Eventually, a bed of cork fenders was made for it, and it was pulled upside down by a team of men working behind the shelter of a sand bank. The detonator was found to be seized into the mine and could not be unscrewed. Somehow, a line was then secured to a crowbar, which was thrust through a ring on the detonator. By using a gang of men to jerk on this line while the mine rocked about alarmingly on its bed of cork, the detonator was at last removed and the mine made safe. Everyone involved had acted very coolly, dangerously close to a lethal and poorly understood weapon.

The success of German submarine minelayers led the British to follow suit. Soon, two of the large and extremely effective new British E class submarines, *E.24* and *E.41*, were fitted for mine laying. Originally, it had been suggested that mines should be ejected from the torpedo tubes, but this very much restricted the size of the mine, so vertical mine-laying tubes were fitted to the boats, and a special mine with Hertz type horns was designed to fit them. Twenty mines could be carried as well as torpedo armament. These mines also had a new type of ·mooring and depth control system incorporating a hydrostat and pilot wire. Successful trials led to the conversion of *E.34*, *E.45*, *E.46* and *E.51* for mine laying. *E24* successfully put down the first British submarine-laid minefield in the Bight in March 1916. Unfortunately, she was lost shortly afterwards for reasons that were never determined. Now that mines had 'come in from the cold' and formed an important part of British naval strategy, other ideas for offensive mine laying were adopted, of which the most effective was the conversion of one of the new, fast destroyer flotilla leaders into a minelayer. *Abdiel* (1,600 tons) could make thirty-four knots and was the forerunner of a generation of extremely successful British purpose-built fast mine-laying craft. She replaced the old cruisers and with the help of the converted merchantmen she successfully laid the majority of the mines in the Bight from summer 1916 onwards.

The appearance of the aggressive Scheer as commander of the High Seas Fleet led Jellicoe to believe that more exercises would be conducted by the Germans in the Bight early in 1916 and it was important to replace the original minefields, which had now mostly been swept, with the more effective new mines and to extend them, so that German fleet exercises would be fraught with danger. In fact, few such exercises were conducted, possibly because Scheer was aware of the danger that the new minefields presented.

Even more important than the offensive fields close to the German coast was the vital need to check U-boat operations, especially those originating from the Belgian coast. In April

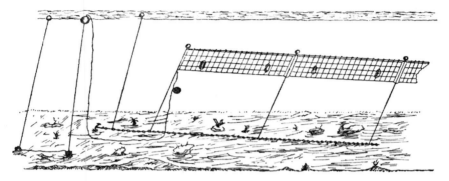

Figure 13: The electro-contact mined net. These were designed primarily to catch submarines and were moored off the Belgian coast in 1916. A submarine striking the net would detonate a nearby mine electrically. It was backed up by a line of deep and shallow contact mines. The laying of these nets in waters close to the enemy coast in 1916 was a considerable achievement.

1916 a massive operation involving *Princess Margaret*, *Biarritz*, *Orvieto* and *Paris*, accompanied by destroyers, six trawlers, a number of drifters and two monitors was undertaken. Forty miles of deep contact mines, specially adapted to be fatal to submarines, and fifteen miles of mined nets (see Figure 13) were moored between the River Scheldt and Ostend so as to form a barrier to submarines and surface craft. The operation was not without excitement. On one occasion the drifters that were detailed to watch the nets came under attack from German seaplanes, one of which was shot down. On another, the covering destroyers were in action with three German destroyers out of Zeebrugge, who skilfully led their opponents into the range of shore batteries. Several British ships were hit and damaged before the monitors caught up with the action and the destroyers were able to withdraw. The anti-submarine mines laid during this operation contained about 65 lb of explosive and were electrically detonated on contact with the supporting net. This required a battery that was housed in a buoy moored at the seaward end of the nets. The battery needed changing from time to time and this, too, was a hazardous operation, as it often meant picking up the buoy when under fire from nearby enemy forces. The barrier was a formidable obstacle and as soon as it was in place the watching drifters had the satisfaction of witnessing the destruction of two U-boats. Like most successful minefields this barrage was constantly patrolled so as to deter enemy sweepers.

Occasionally British ability to read German signals would have an important impact on mine laying operations. *UC.75* for example was detected when she passed down Channel and her position roughly fixed by radio direction finding. Her call sign enabled the British to identify her as a mine layer. Her next signal indicated that she was heading for an area near Queenstown in Ireland. Obviously she intended to lay her mines there and sneak home. Sweepers were alerted and the field swept as soon as it had been laid. *UC.30* was even more unlucky. She was located passing down Channel in April 1917. Off the Scillies she reported again, and this time she stated that she had severe engine problems. She passed slowly round the west coast of Ireland, reporting again off the Fastnet, and then again a week later off the Hebrides. Here she met *UC.50*, then proceeded slowly into the North Sea. British minelayers were alerted and a string of mines laid across her likely track. Another signal from her gave a more accurate location and more mines were placed in her way. *UC.30* never got home, almost certainly due to a mine strike. In October of the same year *U.75* met the same fate when she ran onto a mine laid by the British submarine *E.51*. *E.51* had been directed to the spot where *U.75* had arranged to part with escorting patrol boats covering her exit from her home port. *U.22* together with an escorting destroyer *S16* and a trawler, *Doggerbank,* were lost soon afterwards due to mines put down by surface ships. These incidents illustrate the vital role Room 40 with its radio location stations and its access to German codes played in the war.

During 1916 a number of further improvements were made to British moored mines, which were to culminate in an entirely new Hertz horn-type mine (the 'H.II mine' – see Figure 14) containing 320 lb of explosive and fitted with a plummet type depth-finding device (the Mark VIII and Mark IX sinkers). There were four horns on the upper hemisphere and two on the lower, to increase effectiveness against submarines. The mine could be laid in up to 200 fathoms of

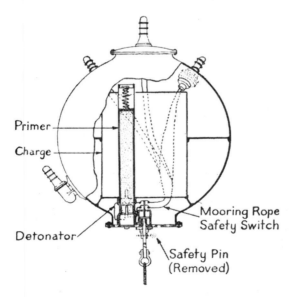

Figure 14: The British H.II mine. These were introduced in 1916/17 and were far better than the Naval Spherical type. They could be laid at up to 20 knots. There was one Hertz horn on top, three on the upper hemisphere and two on the lower. They could be laid in very deep water – up to 200 fathoms (later increased to 600).

water. The plummet-type sinker was arranged so that the mines could be laid at high speed (20 knots) (see Figure 3). Maximum depth below the surface was 50 fathoms – deep enough to trap submarines of the time. The first batch of these was laid in September 1917. At last, Britain had a really effective moored mine. This mine remained in service into the Second World War. Accuracy of positioning was improved by means of a system of wires fed out behind the mine-laying vessel, which enabled her to space the mines correctly and also to chart their position precisely. This was becoming extremely important as the increasing number of British mines distributed about the North Sea were a serious hazard to our own fleet operations and to the minelayers themselves. Fleet anchorage protection from U-boats also received a lot of attention, and a magnetic submarine detection system was developed for harbour defence.

By now, it was clear that the High Seas Fleet was unlikely to give battle in the North Sea again. A consequence of this was that the Grand Fleet would be unlikely to have to enter the German Bight to chase the enemy. Churchill's hare-brained schemes for attacking Heligoland or the German mainland coast had long since been abandoned. This led the Admiralty to conclude that extensive mining in the North Sea was unlikely to hamper important Grand Fleet operations, and its outcome would be to increase the effectiveness of the allied blockade of Germany, and make life more difficult for her dreaded U-boats. A new division of the Admiralty, the Mines Division, under the experienced leadership of Captain Lionel Preston, was established by Jellicoe in 1916, almost as soon as he took over as First Sea Lord. This marked the start of a new chapter in the story of British mining activities.

By the beginning of 1917, British mine stocks were being increased to no fewer than 100,000 mines of all types, a staggering advance on the 4,000 available at the start of the war, and an increasing proportion of this stock was of the new, improved type. One heavy cruiser, six light cruisers, twelve destroyers and a number of small coastal motor boats, were added to the mine-laying force. Technology was also improving fast. An acoustic attachment was designed and fitted to some moored mines, enabling them to explode if an enemy vessel passed close to the mine. At the same time some ground mines, used in shallow water, were fitted with a magnetic firing device for the same purpose – these were the first magnetic mines ever deployed. The need to lay anti-submarine mines in waters subject to strong tidal currents, such as the Dover Strait, resulted in the provision of extra heavy sinkers, and also a safety device so that if they did inadvertently float close to the surface, thus becoming a danger to friendly coastal craft, the mines were disarmed. This was the year in which the situation as regards U-boats became extremely critical. Having failed to mount any really effective action against the Grand Fleet, the enemy concentrated on using their submarine force to destroy Britain's maritime communications and force her to quit the war. In this they very nearly succeeded, Britain's food supplies being reduced to a few week's requirement. As there was still no effective means of detecting submarines under water, the job of handling the submarine menace devolved mainly on the mine-laying force. Mines could destroy submarines and mine defences and barriers could force them into narrow channels in which they could be intercepted and dealt with by surface vessels. Deep mines or a mined net could force them to the surface where they could fall victim to destroyers.

The first suggestion, put forward by Beatty, who had taken over from Jellicoe as commander of the Grand Fleet, was to lay a barrier of deep and shallow mines across the whole mouth of the Bight. This would have involved a barrier about 169 miles long, and would have required 60,000 mines – over half the proposed stock. This scheme was not fully carried out, instead a series of fields were laid in the hope that the enemy would believe that the barrier was complete. These, of course, were a severe problem for neutral shipping and, eventually, the Dutch Government was permitted to moor lightships in strategic places to allow safe passage. At the same time a barrage of mines and nets was put down across the entrance to the Dover Strait, between the South Goodwin Sand and Dunkirk. This consisted of a mined nets supported by buoys, backed by three lines of deep mines. The nets were regularly patrolled by trawlers and these were backed up by the destroyers and heavy ships of the Dover Patrol. At the same time, coastal motor boats were used to extend and thicken up the mine barrages off Lowestoft and the barrier off Zebrugge was extended. These barriers, as we shall see, were never very effective due to the vulnerability of the nets and the inability of patrols to spot and engage U-boats in darkness. As was to be expected, German minesweeping forces worked hard to sweep these fields, but by 1917 it appears that they were becoming over extended and their efforts began to flag. They found it very difficult to sweep fields distant from the German coasts, largely because of the constant activities of Harwich-based British light forces. This often meant they had to be supported by heavy German ships, which were consequently at risk from mines and submarines. They were able, however, to keep open the swept channels, which allowed their own U-boats and destroyers to continue to operate. German destroyers were also successful in sinking the buoys that supported the mined nets, thus rendering them ineffective. Constant drifter patrols had to be maintained to keep the nets in position, and the drifters themselves were, of course, at extreme risk from mines and from destroyers. German records suggest that throughout 1917 an average of twenty-three U-boats per month passed through or over the nets, mines and obstructions that had been laid to deter them.

As the submarine menace became more severe, more drastic measures were called for and it was determined to close off both exits from the North Sea completely. A glance at the map will show what a gigantic operation this would be. The new barriers, if completed, would mark a decisive change in the role of the Royal Navy, from a force primarily concerned with working towards a major fleet action, which everyone had expected in the early years of the war, into one whose principal task was to deal with the submarine menace. It was a momentous change and one that was to re-ignite some of the bitter controversy and rivalries that had riven the service in the during the infamous Fisher v Beresford disputes at the turn of the century.

Admiral Lord Charles Beresford had been very much a traditional naval officer and had hated and despised Fisher and his reforms. The controversy that raged between the two in the early years of the twentieth century had split the Navy down the middle, with Jellicoe firmly in the Fisher camp. One of the protagonists was Roger Keyes, now a rear admiral, and serving in the planning division of the Admiralty, much to his disgust, as he would have preferred an active appointment. The other was Vice Admiral Sir Reginald Bacon, the admiral commanding Dover. Jellicoe, the First Sea Lord was, like Bacon, one of the 'Fish Pond' as Fisher's protégés were called, and was inclined to favour Bacon's cause. He considered Keyes quite unsuitable for a staff posting, but was unable to prevent it. Beatty, commanding the Grand Fleet, had much more in common with Keyes. The most contested matter involved in this confrontation was the plan for building a really effective mine barrage across the English Channel, which would make it totally impassable to submarines. Plans for such a barrage had been submitted to Bacon early in the war by Captain Munro, a capable officer who had successfully built anti-submarine defences for the fleet anchorages at Scapa and Cromarty. Bacon rejected Munro's plans out of hand. He wrote 'A glance at the scheme was sufficient to condemn it. Captain Munro's scheme would not last a single tide' – rather a cavalier rejection of the plans of an officer who had successfully erected a similar structure in the fierce waters around northern Scotland. Instead, Bacon relied on, as we have seen, the mined nets in the southern North Sea and off the Goodwins. While these had been initially successful, they were too prone to be swept by the enemy and difficult and dangerous for British patrols to cover effectively, being so close to German held Belgian ports. Nevertheless, Bacon maintained that his scheme was effective and pointed to the extremely low casualty rate of cross Channel ships during his tenure as officer commanding Dover.

Unfortunately for Bacon, Keyes obtained a copy of the papers of a mine-laying submarine, our old friend from Waterford, *U.C.44*. These made it clear that twenty to thirty U-boats a month were getting down the Channel past Bacon's defences so as to wreak havoc among the shipping in the Western Approaches. Orders to the U-boat commanders stated clearly:

It is best to pass this (The Dover Barrage) on the surface: if forced to dive go down to 40 metres. As far as possible pass through the area between Hoofden and Cherbourg without being observed and without stopping; on the other hand boats which in exceptional circumstances go round the north of Scotland are to let themselves be seen as freely as possible in order to mislead the English.

In other words, their orders were to sneak down Channel unseen so that the British thought their barrier was effective, and bluff the Royal Navy into thinking that they were all going round Scotland.

Bacon was made aware of the content of *U.C.44*'s orders and asked what he intended to do about it. He replied defensively, emphasizing the need to keep the Dover Strait open for use by his warships and submitting plans for a new deep minefield between the Varne Bank, in mid Channel and Cap Griz Nez. He saw no reason to cover this with any force stronger than a few small patrol boats. The situation, however, as regards the submarine war, was now critical. It was a question of 'beat the subs or lose the war', and it did not seem that Bacon was achieving the necessary level of success. In October 1917, over 350,000 tonnes of merchant shipping was lost to submarines in the Channel and the Western Approaches alone, and almost all the offending boats must have passed down the Channel past the Dover defences. Sir Eric Geddes, now the First Lord of the Admiralty, called a meeting of senior naval officers and civil and military engineers to thrash out the issue of closing the Channel to submarines completely. All sorts of ideas, including large acoustic and magnetic mines, and massive floating towers were discussed and eventually a sub committee chaired by Bacon's rival, Keyes, was appointed. The committee visited Dover and were taken to sea in the powerful destroyer *Swift*, which promptly ran over one of the mined nets. Fortunately, it didn't explode but the committee noted the large lighted buoy from which it was suspended. Obviously, this would be an easy target for an enemy destroyer. Also, they remarked that if the impact of the 1,800-ton 30-knot destroyer did not set off the mines in the net, there was little chance of a small sub doing so. Bacon responded to the committee's criticisms with a scheme to build a new class of heavily armoured vessel, possibly developed from heavy barges, and powerful land-based searchlights to cover the Channel minefields.

The committee made its interim report on 29 November 1917, suggesting a much-enhanced barrier of deep and shallow mines, heavily patrolled, as a first step that could be undertaken immediately. This would be supplemented by heavy mined nets. The patrols would be provided with very powerful searchlights and 'Brock's Flares' so as to be effective by night as well as by day. While this was being put in place, new systems would be rapidly developed to make the defences even more effective. It was critical of the measures taken by Bacon up to date and of his decision to abandon a net barrage between Folkestone and Griz Nez, which had been commenced in 1915 by his predecessor.

Bacon, although he accepted the report, did very little to implement it. He was particularly reluctant to expose ships under his command to the danger of attack by making them burn flares and searchlights during the night, and he kept on delaying the deployment of the cross-Channel net barrage. This tardiness gave Keyes his opening. Naval intelligence reported at least thirty-five U-boat transits of the Channel in the period 1 November to 9 December and the very highest levels of the government were now involved in the issue. Early in December a definite order was sent to Bacon to undertake the proposed measures as the highest priority, even if it meant abandoning other activities. He visited the Admiralty on 18 December and attended what must have been a frosty meeting, during which he gave many reasons why he was so reluctant to patrol the minefields and nets with the modern destroyers at his disposal, but eventually agreed to do so and to order the patrols to use illumination at night. This was immediately successful, as that very night *U-59* was illuminated while crossing the minefield by night and dived straight onto a mine, which destroyed her.

Keyes's committee submitted its final report before the year end. Two professors, Bragg and McLennan, had worked quickly to establish the feasibility of a hydrophone system that would detect the movement of U-boats in the Channel. Amusingly, their experiments had been conducted in the Firth of Forth, where they were puzzled by serious interference with their system, which seemed to disappear only in the early hours of the morning. The perplexed professors spent over a week pondering this problem until someone realized that the interference exactly coincided with the schedule of the Edinburgh to Leith electric tramway, many miles away, which just happened to create interference on the selected frequency. The report called for a deep minefield consisting of contact mines at various depths, which would be heavily patrolled by ships using searchlights and flares constantly at night. To the east of this would be a surface minefield electrically controlled by an operator who would be warned of the presence of a submarine by the hydrophone system. Ten enormous concrete towers would also be fitted with 4-inch guns and searchlights and placed at intervals across the Folkestone–Griz Nez passage; the operators of the electrically controlled mines would be accommodated in these. Heavy steel nets would be strung between them. Also, indicating loops should be laid to eastwards and westwards of the barrier to give early warning, and ships should be moored at two-mile intervals across the Channel to supplement the towers. Large magnetic ground mines would be placed in the shallower areas. Merchant ships were confined to narrow channels swept daily and heavily patrolled.

Had it been completed, this arrangement would have probably been 100 per cent submarine proof, but it was not finished when hostilities ceased. The most remarkable feature of it, the towers, was commenced in Shoreham Harbour, but only one of these was almost completed by the war end. This was eventually used as a lighthouse and can be seen today off Hayling Island in Hampshire, the massive and forbidding Nab Tower.

Lloyd George, the Prime Minister, was desperately concerned about the submarine war and had lost confidence in Jellicoe to solve the problems related to it. He encouraged Geddes to replace him, and on 24 December, Admiral Sir Rosslyn Wemyss was appointed in his place. Wemyss lost no time in turning his attention to the Channel barrage and on 28 December called Keyes into his office and said, 'Well Roger you have talked a hell of a lot about what ought to be done in the Dover area, and now you must go and do it.' Thus, the dilatory Bacon was replaced and vigorous work on the barrage commenced.

Immediately, the deep and shallow minefields were set in hand and, most importantly, the ships of the Dover Patrol were equipped with flares and ordered to patrol intensively above the minefields illuminating them brilliantly at night. Normally there would be four destroyers, fourteen armed trawlers, sixty drifters, two large minesweepers and about four motor boats patrolling over the minefields at any one time. Numbers of ships might be increased in periods of poor visibility. A monitor with 12-inch guns would be stationed in mid-Channel to act as a hub for the patrol. This intensive patrolling with brilliant illumination was the action that Bacon had most bitterly opposed, claiming that his existing defences were almost 100 per cent submarine proof. He had

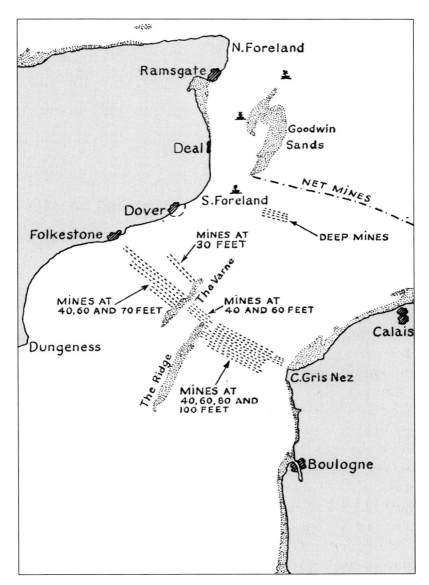

Chart 4: The Folkestone–Griz Nez barrage in 1918. In spite of all these hazards, U-boats still managed to pass up and down the Channel.

been concerned for the safety of his ships operating at night, showing powerful lights. Practice proved that these fears were not entirely misplaced.

Staff officers who had worked under Bacon had never been told of the information gleaned by naval Intelligence about U-boats still passing down Channel or about the orders retrieved from *U-44*. When Keyes informed them of the real situation they were naturally appalled. In truth, Bacon was a highly competent technician and could be a bold and effective leader, but he was stubborn and made enemies easily. 'The Streaky One' as he was called in the service, had really painted himself into a corner by refusing to accept or act on criticism of his management of the Dover anti-submarine offensive, and his dismissal had become overdue. Keyes' new policy soon began to take effect; four boats were destroyed by being forced to dive into minefields in January and February (*U-35*, *U-109*, *UB-38* and *UC-50*), forcing the Germans to route most of their subs around Scotland.

Retribution, however, was not long in coming. On 14 February a strong patrol of fast German destroyers appeared among the patrolling drifters and trawlers, unchallenged by the British warships present. As Bacon had predicted, they made use of the lights displayed by the little ships to sink a trawler and seven drifters and damage an Admiralty paddler. Keyes was furious, as were the RNMR crews of the surviving drifters. The very next day a U-boat shelled Dover then laid a pattern of shallow mines to catch any ship sent out to catch her. The attack was insulting, but did little damage and the mines were soon dealt with. Although these actions were very disturbing for the Dover Patrol, they did show that the new tactics were causing the U-boats severe problems and this only led Keyes to redouble his efforts to complete the barrage and increase the intensity of his surface patrols. A reward of £1,000 was instituted for any fishing vessel that managed to force a U-boat to dive down onto a minefield. Constant pressure was applied to the Admiralty to provide the Dover Patrol with more destroyers and more fast torpedo boats, as frequently drifters and trawlers heard submarines on the surface, but were too slow to have a hope of catching them and forcing them to dive. Keyes took his appeal as far as the Prime Minister, who he met on a cross-Channel voyage, and very gradually his force was increased and the intensity of the patrols built up and the mines exacted a continual toll of U-boats. *U-79* was sunk in April and *UB-55* was an early victim of the first of the acoustic indicator loops installed during that month. In May, two more subs, returning from the Western Approaches were forced to dive and hit mines. These were *UB-31* and *UC-78*, the latter being the victim of a smart piece of spotting by a small airship (a 'blimp'). Both boats had been creeping along at periscope depth hoping to scrape over the mines when they were detected. Losses continued into June, by which time the convoy system and the mines and obstructions laid in the Channel and in northern waters had blunted the U-boat threat quite effectively. At long last the barrage was becoming a major factor in the U-boat war, the contest that Britain simply had to win.

In August a further development in aggressive mine laying took place when the invaluable *Abdiel* and five consorts put down a very effective field of magnetic ground mines off Zeebrugge. These immediately claimed an enemy destroyer, and also seem to have destroyed a detail of minesweepers sent to remove them without understanding their nature. During the same month *U-109* fell victim to a controlled mine detonated by an operator on shore after she had been detected by an indicator loop. She had been trying to sneak through the narrow channel kept open for merchant shipping, on the surface, very close to a merchant ship. An alert operator had detected the high frequency vibrations of her diesels and detonated his mines just clear of the merchantman. The regime of tireless patrolling by small warships and fishing boats, allied to new technology, was making the Channel passage almost impossible for the enemy, even before the tower and net barrage was in place. The last U-boat to be caught in the minefields was *UB-103* on 16 September. By that time the combination of the convoy system, introduced in 1917, and the barrages had finally won the U-boat war for the Allies.

A graphic account of a passage through the minefields written by Werner Fürbringer survives. He was bringing his damaged boat home after an unsatisfactory cruise in the Western Approaches during which he had suffered from constant torpedo failures:

> By the time I judged it safe to surface it was dark, but what was this ahead? The boat was bathed in the glare of five or six huge searchlights trained on us from the direction in which the barrier lay. The obvious conclusion was that the British wanted us to run submerged to elude the light barrier because they had set some ghastly new trap below. In a heavy swell a breakthrough on the surface could usually be risked for the boat would rarely be visible, even in the searchlight beams, but tonight the sea was calm. I had no choice but to do what the English wanted and submerge, but I would not do them the favour of going deep as they obviously wished. I would trim the boat to run as close to the surface as I could and allow nothing to force me deeper, navigating neatly between the patrol boats above and the minefield below.

We set off on the surface for the searchlight barrier, not diving until blinded by the glare. I trimmed the boat so the keel was thirteen metres below the surface, the highest point of the conning tower then being five metres below the water. I knew there were bound to be mines here moored below eight metres where they were harmless to steamers but lethal to U-boats.

Finally, by my reckoning we were directly before the barrier. Here the mines would definitely be set shallow and we would have to hang only inches below the surface. I trimmed the boat to eight metres so that the bridge was almost breaking through. Then came the ticklish part.

I raised the periscope half a metre above the surface. It was bathed in light and I could see nothing. After a while I got used to the glare and managed to pick out where the searchlight ships were. One was stationed on our starboard hand and we would have to pass him very close. For a few seconds the searchlight trained away and I could make out the lines of a large destroyer. He changed course and bore down on us suddenly, his beam shining directly into my periscope eye. In the light I could not see him, and I had been so cautious with the periscope I doubted he could have detected us, but he might have heard us. I retracted the tube and whispered for the revolutions of the motors to be put at minimum. The grinding of the destroyer's propellers grew louder but after listening for some time we decided that his engines were at slow ahead, and soon he turned away.

Nevertheless the British concentration must have known we were about for no sooner had we left the first bag of tricks astern than another presented itself. Behind the line of searchlight destroyers the night was suddenly illuminated bright as day when another group of patrol vessels fired star shell simultaneously. These vessels were probably blinded by their own pyrotechnics and were a matter of no concern to us. Our worry was the more distant warships which we suspected would be closely examining the backcloth of light for the outline of an enemy submarine.

Once again we were in an abysmal situation. Below us the mines, astern a sea of light against which the silhouette of a submarine would be instantly visible...I blest my lucky star that I had read the situation correctly and decided to remain submerged.

Fürbringer's boat escaped the horrors of that night and made port safely, only to be rammed and sunk on its next voyage. The episode illustrates how a skilled commander could avoid the barriers if he kept his head and had good luck, but it was not easy. Holding a submarine at a precise depth, as he did, requires a highly skilled crew and excellent co-ordination. As the war went on and experienced commanders and crews were eroded, casualty rates in these situations like this increased. In 1918 this barrage and its attendant patrols accounted for eighteen U-boats.

The great German land offensive in the summer of 1918 posed a new problem for naval planners. It seemed that the British and Belgian armies in northern France were close to defeat and the enemy might be able to drive a wedge between them and the French, isolating them on the Channel coast. This would have been militarily and politically disastrous and it was decided that the British Army should close with the French, abandoning, if necessary, the Channel ports as far as Cherbourg. This presented the horrible prospect of the eastern part of the Channel becoming open to German warships, operating out or the Belgian ports.

Hurriedly, plans were made for a programme of intensive mining of the whole area with a fearsome combination of deep and shallow mines covered by coastal artillery on the northern side and by ships using marked channels to the south. Fortunately, the offensive was halted and dramatically reversed when the over-extended German armies met British forces re-supplied and stiffened with Dominion troops.

Far more challenging than sealing off the Channel was the problem of closing the northern approach to the North Sea. The barrage would be far too distant from Germany for their forces to have any chance of sweeping it or of interfering seriously with its construction. Nevertheless, it would be a mammoth undertaking and could only be accomplished with US help and materials. The US had entered the war on the Allied side, and American troops were being shipped across the Atlantic to join the French forces on the right of the Allied lines. The US Navy, however, although it was a powerful and modern force, had nothing much to do. Five of the American dreadnought battleships joined the Grand Fleet at Scapa, where, like the British, they had no chance of any action as the Germans were clearly not going to venture out of harbour. US destroyers did useful work in escorting Atlantic convoys, but although this led to a lot of steaming, there was very little action, as U-boats had learnt to keep well clear of escorted convoys. There was one area where the US could play a major part, however – the production and laying of mines. Quickly, they were allotted a major part in the planning and implementation of what came to be called the Northern Barrage.

The barrage was a particularly suitable undertaking for the US Navy as it was designed to prevent enemy warships from venturing into the Atlantic where they could attack troopers carrying US soldiers to France. It also enabled the US to make good use of its colossal manufacturing base to design and build mines, which it was thought would be suitable for the barrage, in enormous quantities.

The first idea considered was a barrage running northwards from the Belgian coast then turning east so as to meet the Jutland coast about half way up the Jutland peninsula. This presented several difficulties:

- It would make it impossible for the Grand Fleet to chase any German raiders into the Bight.
- It would be relatively easy for the enemy to reach and sweep.
- It would not prevent boats exiting from the Baltic.

Another idea was to place the barrage so that it ran from Thurso north-eastwards to the Shetlands then eastwards to the coast of Norway. This was rejected on the grounds of the bad holding ground and strong tidal currents. Also, the depth of water off the relevant part of the Norwegian coast was too great for mine laying (most mines were restricted to 50 fathoms).

Eventually, a modification of this scheme was adopted, the line chosen being further south and leaving the Pentland Firth uncovered. (It was considered to be too turbulent for submarines to pass submerged, and narrow enough to be relatively easy to patrol with destroyers.) The reasons for choosing this line were numerous, the most important being:

- The entrance to the Baltic would be closed.
- It was too far from Germany for sweepers to reach unless covered by heavy ships.
- It did not restrict Grand Fleet operations in the North Sea
- U-boats damaged in the barrage would have a long and dangerous haul home.

This line was slightly shorter than either of the other proposals, but it was, nevertheless, a colossal undertaking, involving putting down some 70,000 mines covering a line 240 miles long. Originally, it had been intended to use entirely the new British H.II mines, but not enough were available early in 1917, and when the US entered the war in April it was agreed that they should provide a significant proportion of the mines and of the mine-laying effort. A squadron of American minelayers consisting of two converted cruisers and ten converted merchant vessels was based at Inverness and in the Cromarty Firth. The merchant vessels were mostly quite large ships with a capacity of 830 mines.

The original intention was to lay a field of both deep and shallow mines in the centre section of the barrage, and to declare its presence to neutral countries. On the wings of this central field deep mines only would be laid. These would be lethal to submerged submarines but would allow merchantmen to pass in safety. The wings would be patrolled to catch any sub trying to pass on the surface. It was hoped that Norway could be persuaded to allow patrol craft to base themselves on a Norwegian port. Work on an efficient system of hydrophones to locate U-boats near the barrier was pushed forward. However, the involvement of the US Navy soon introduced new technology into the picture. The Americans were enthusiastic about the possibilities of the barrage, and its role in keeping safe the numerous trans-Atlantic troopers. (In fact, not one was lost during the entire war.) They came up with a new method for actuation of mines known as the Antenna System (see Figure 15). Long antennas projected upwards and downwards from the mine so that it was effective over a very wide range of depths. A ship striking the antennas would set up an electrical circuit that would detonate the mine. Horns were also fitted to the

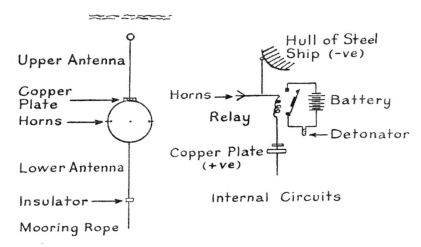

Figure 15: An antenna mine as originally conceived. The long vertical antennas were designed to catch submarines. If they had worked effectively, they would have drastically reduced the number of deep and shallow mines needed to complete the Northern Barrage. These mines worked on the principle of the steel hull of a passing ship and a copper plate on the antenna setting up an electric current, using the sea water as an electrolyte. In practice, these mines were not very satisfactory, because they tended to explode prematurely due to insulation faults, and because the lower antennas had to be removed.

body of the mine to trigger it in the event of a direct hit. The vertical distance covered by an antenna mine was 140 feet, enabling one antenna mine to do the work of four conventional contact mines moored one above the other. In the end, 15 rows of mines were specified, each row consisting of mines 45 feet, 160 feet and 240 feet deep.

Early in March 1918 work on the barrage started in earnest, the Americans laying the centre section with their new mines, and the British working on the wings with conventional contact mines. A problem soon arose when the sloop *Gaillardia* struck a mine in an area that was supposed to be covered by deep mines only. It was then found that many of the mines in the area were laid too shallow, and they had to be swept up and re-laid. The system of patrolling the wings of the field was soon found to be unworkable, and it was decided to cover them with shallow mines as well as deep. To achieve this, the old battleship *London* and a cruiser were converted into minelayers, as the existing fleet did not have enough range to cover the area close to the Norwegian coast.

Both British and American mines suffered from problems of 'countermining', that is to say one mine exploding and setting off others, especially in rough seas. This was countered by sowing the mines in groups of four, each mine 120 feet from its neighbour and separating each group of mines by a distance of 150 feet. In theory, this made little difference to the effectiveness of barrier but did reduce the danger of a chain reaction.

Some early problems with the effectiveness of the barrage were encountered. Firstly, it was decided that the seventy foot upper antennas were too long because a U-boat could survive an exploding mine at any distance of more than thirty-five feet from the hull. This was discovered in June 1918 when a radio report from *U-86* was intercepted. She indicated that she had triggered a mine and survived. Also, the lower antennas were abandoned as they proved impractical, continually causing the mines to explode prematurely. This meant that some mines had to be re-laid and the depth set at forty-five feet instead of eighty feet. Secondly, it became clear that U-boats were skirting around the northern end of the barrage, running through Norwegian territorial waters. Eventually, the Norwegian Government, which had balked at the idea of allowing a British base for patrol boats to be established in one of the fjords, agreed to allow the Royal Navy to extend its minefield, consisting of both deep and shallow mines, right up to its shoreline. In fact, by the end of the war this was not completed and subs were still getting past the northern end of the barrage in Norwegian territorial waters. Had the northern flank been finished, the only passage into and out of the North Sea would have been a swept and heavily patrolled area close to the Orkneys.

In the end, the effectiveness of the Northern Barrage was a disappointment. At the most, six U-boats were probably destroyed in it, and a considerable number passed through undamaged. The water was too deep for effective netting and the distance too great for intensive patrolling like that operated in the Channel. To be successful, any obstacle to movement must be covered by fire and the barrage was not. There were simply not enough small ships and aircraft available to cover the whole length of the barrage in all weather. In theory, it was calculated that a U-boat had a 66 per cent chance of getting through unscathed if submerged, and a 33 per cent chance on the surface, but, in fact, its chances were much higher than this. The mines often did not work correctly and the modifications that had to be made to the antenna mines reduced their effectiveness against submarines running deep under water. At some points the sea in which the barrage was laid was 150 fathoms deep, far deeper than it had previously been thought possible to lay mines at all. In spite of its shortcomings, the barrage was a massive organizational and technical achievement. Some 57,000 mines were laid by the Americans and a further 14,000 by the British. While it was certainly not a decisive factor in the defeat of the U-boat, it undoubtedly made their life far more difficult. Its cost had been formidable – about £30 million, (about £5 million for each boat sunk). But as Joseph Daniels, the US Secretary of the Navy, pointed out, the war was costing more than £30m every day, so if it shortened the conflict by one day it was worthwhile.

The Northern and Channel Barrages were not the only mine-laying activities undertaken during the last year of the war. It was discovered early in 1918, long before the barrage was in place, that U-boats were operating out of the Baltic and getting into the Atlantic through the Kattegat, and this had to be countered before the northern barrage was ready. There was a danger that mining the Kattegat would bring Sweden into the war on the German side, but it was eventually agreed that the Swedes would tolerate deep laid anti-submarine mines, which were no danger to surface shipping. The operation involved laying mines in the enemy dominated waters and the fast minelayers *Abdiel* and *Princess Margaret*, accompanied by three cruisers and a strong back-up force, were sent to lay deep mines in the shipping lane.

This was accomplished in two operations, but it seems that many of the mines exploded prematurely. At the same time the US minelayer *Baltimore* put down a small field of H.II mines in the north western approaches to the Irish Sea. Again, some difficulties were encountered with the depth setting of the mines, but the field was effective in reducing U-boat activity. Operations continued in the Bight, conducted in the main by a flotilla of mine-laying destroyers of various vintages, but all fast enough to get out of trouble should they be discovered. There were, however, now so many mines in the area that a scheme to mine the approaches to the German naval bases with dense new fields had to be abandoned, as to reach their destination the minelayers would have to be preceded by a large minesweeping force. The destroyer *Ferret* was used to lay a field of oscillating Leon-type mines in an area frequented by enemy ships, but these do not seem to have been effective and this type of mine was abandoned entirely. Another novel device used in the Bight was the delayed-release sinker. These were used in areas which the enemy would find fairly easy to sweep. The mines would be held inactive on the bottom when they were laid, and then would be released at varying intervals. Thus sweepers would never know when a field had been completely cleared, presenting another difficulty for an over-extended minesweeping force. (The Germans had already made use of delayed-action mines in British shipping lanes.)

These fields made enemy operations in the Bight extremely hazardous. Twenty-eight destroyers, seventy smaller craft, and at least four U-boats came to grief in the Bight as a result of British mining, and battleships and battle cruisers were severely damaged on several occasions. The most prolific mine-laying vessels were *Princess Margaret*, which laid over 10,000 mines in the Bight during the war, and the ubiquitous *Abdiel*, which entered the Bight on no fewer than sixty-eight occasions. It is worth remembering that these expeditions took the minelayers into waters close to enemy bases, often in bad weather. The very highest standards of navigation were required, as any mistake would be likely to take the ship over a friendly or possibly an enemy minefield. These voyages were often undertaken in thick weather, which gave some protection from enemy activity, but meant that navigation had to depend on dead reckoning and on taking soundings with an armed lead. Sometimes the enemy would correctly guess the area to be mined and would set a trap for the mine-laying vessels. The destroyers *Kale*, *Vehement* and *Ariel* were lost in this way, for example, in 1918.

In the southern section of the North Sea, 400 magnetic ground mines were laid in shoal water by destroyers and by coastal motor boats. These lay on the bottom and were actuated by the magnetic field generated by any ship passing overhead (see Figure 16). They could only be used in shallow water. Off Ostend and Zeebrugge they constituted another hazard for light German forces and U-boats. At the same time conventional mining in this sector continued, mostly carried

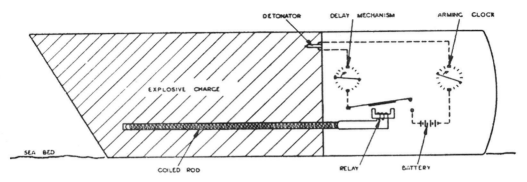

Figure 16: A magnetic ground mine. Very advanced for its day, this type of mine would be very effective against submarines in shallow water. They were too late to play a major role in the First World War.

out by the motor boats operating at night and at high speed.

In late summer of 1918, as more H.II mines came off the production lines, a new defensive minefield was laid off the Yorkshire coast to deter submarines and surface raiders. Controlled minefields around headlands and in the Thames Estuary were reinforced.

The last fling of the High Seas Fleet, planned for October/November 1918, was to be a 'death ride' into the mouth of the Thames to try to do the maximum of damage before the war ended. It never took place because the underfed and disillusioned German seamen refused to take their ships to sea. If it had gone ahead the defensive minefields, many of them unknown to German planners, would have been a formidable obstacle.

By the time of the Armistice, in November 1918, British mine laying had evolved from a sadly neglected sector of British naval activity into a key area of the Royal Navy's strategy. It had become crucial in the battle against the submarine menace. Industrial mass production of mines in the UK and in the US allowed them to be deployed on a hitherto unimaginable scale. Some 128,000 mines were laid by Britain and over 57,000 by the US Navy, almost half the British mines being placed by submarines, small warships or converted ferries in the hostile waters of the eastern North Sea and the Kattegat. British and US mines sunk 150 enemy warships, including approximately 40 U-boats. (Frequently, it is impossible to determine the cause of U-boat losses.) Even more important than the numbers of U-boats actually sunk by mines, was the inconvenience and difficulty caused to them by having their routes to their hunting grounds so heavily obstructed. This often led to missions being curtailed and to boats taking a risky course on the surface, where they fell victim to surface ships.

German forces laid 43,000 mines, many of them by submarine, and mostly in small fields designed to take their opponents by surprise. About 11,000 of these were swept up to the time of the Armistice. Britain lost fewer warships to mines than the Germans, 46 in total, but no fewer than 225 auxiliaries on Admiralty service and 214 minesweepers were destroyed by mines. Some 260 British merchant ships totalling 670,000 tons were also sunk in this way and a further 84 seriously damaged. In total, the number of warships destroyed by mines was greater than those accounted for by gunfire and torpedoes combined.

German mine technology did not change much during the war, except in the development of mines suitable for large submarines, but British mines and minesweeping techniques had to be rapidly developed from a shamefully poor base. It is a tribute to the energy and inventiveness of the mine department at HMS *Vernon* and to British industry that so many effective innovations were made in such a short space of time.

CHAPTER 6

Clearing Up

Mines, of course, remain deadly irrespective of peace treaties or armistices. No fewer than 240,000 mines were scattered about the seas, some in their original position, some having dragged their moorings and settled in a new location, and some drifting freely. These constituted a major danger to shipping after the end of the war. To clear them up an international committee was formed, which included most belligerent and neutral countries, and was eventually joined by the defeated powers. This was called the International Mine Clearance Committee (IMCC) and was organized principally by the Royal Navy. All members carried out mine clearance activities and reported regularly to the IMCC, who issued regular charts and updates showing safe areas and known danger zones. Sweeping was a major operation, almost as unpleasant and difficult in peacetime as it had been during the war. The winter of 1918/19 was cold and unforgiving, so crews had to endure the harshest conditions in constant danger from the sea as well as from the mines themselves, battling with heavy wire hawsers and kites on small ships tossed about by the remorseless waves.

One illustration of this is provided by the sweeper *Penarth*. She was laying buoys to mark the limits of a minefield when she struck a mine and sank. Her captain, the flotilla commander, Commander Brooke, was killed and Lieutenant Wainwright, just released from a prisoner of war camp in Germany, took over. It was a terrible night, dark and windy with driving snow reducing the visibility to almost nothing. Wainwright searched the ship for survivors and then escaped onto a Carley float, an unprotected liferaft, with a handful of men. They were some thirty miles off the Tyne. Waves constantly washed men off the float into the water, and four of them died of exposure before a rescue ship collected Wainwright and the remains of his exhausted band. He was subsequently awarded the Albert Medal for bravery.

The main part of the clearance work was divided between the maritime nations, Germany being responsible for sweeping Heligoland Bight, France the waters off the French and Belgian coasts, America the Northern Barrage and the UK, most of the rest, working through a new organization called the Mine Clearance Service. The service was manned mainly by Royal Navy personnel and fishermen and consisted of 14,500 men and 700 officers at its peak. It was headed by the ubiquitous Lionel Preston, by 1918 with the rank of captain. Five sweepers were lost during these operations and six merchant ships struck mines that had not been swept. After the operation large numbers of sunken unexploded mines remained on the seabed, and were a danger to trawlers, but it proved almost impossible to recover these, and they gradually deteriorated and became harmless with the passage of time.

A particular danger when clearing dense fields was what was known as 'counter mining'. This occurred when exploding one mine would set off others in the vicinity – possibly dangerously close to the sweeper involved. For example, there was a deep and dense anti-submarine minefield off the west coast of Scotland, between Skye and Rathlin Island. A flotilla of sweepers was sent to clear it. Normally, deep fields were left until last, as they did not constitute a serious danger to shipping, but sometimes some of the mines were laid incorrectly and finished up close to the surface. It was determined to skim off any of these shallow mines first, and the sweep began in the normal way. Suddenly, a shallow mine exploded in the sweep and seconds later the whole sea began to erupt in a terrible series of explosions. For three frightening minutes the surface became chaos as deep and shallow mines set each other off, throwing up huge plumes of water. The men in the sweepers waited for the seemingly inevitable disaster when a mine would explode under a ship, blowing it to pieces, but luck was on their side. By the time the explosions had finished the whole field, deep and shallow, had swept itself with every mine detonated, but it was not without cost. Every one of the sweepers had been so battered by the underwater concussions that they had to limp home to the Clyde for major repairs to their bottoms.

One of the most exciting episodes of the Royal Navy's war had been the Zeebrugge Raid, during which locks and port facilities at Zebrugge were blown up by landing parties and block ships were sunk so as to prevent U-boats from getting out of the harbour. Many of the vessels used to perform this tricky operation were coastal motor boats (CMBs) and other small craft with very shallow draft that might be able to land men on the coastal defences and avoid mines laid to defend them. Although a gallant and successful action was fought, it was not very effective as the U-boats soon found that there was a narrow channel that they could use around the block ships. The Germans, however, were clearly afraid that a repeat raid might be in the offing and put down a new field of very shallow mines, awash most of the time, all around the approaches to the Belgian coast. This caused some nasty problems for naval forces that approached the coast in September 1918 after the German Army had been driven headlong from most of Belgium by the advancing British and Belgian Armies.

A force of destroyers and monitors, under Roger Keyes, was given the task of destroying any remaining shore batteries and, if possible, landing a brigade of British troops on the enemy's flank. The harbour at Ostend had been blocked by the retreating Germans, so this attempt was abandoned, but it was renewed on 13 October, a month before the end of the war. It was impossible to bombard the coastal towns without killing many Belgian civilians, but the Navy attempted to clear the minefields by deliberately counter mining with explosives. The technique did not prove very effective. Enemy gun positions on shore were still active and had to be dealt with, mines or no mines. Keyes led the attack in the destroyer *Douglas*, but soon transferred to *Termagant* as she drew three feet less water and would be safer in the minefields. Fire was opened on enemy gun positions, which replied vigorously, forcing the attacking ships to withdraw. Some mines were spotted but were fortunately avoided. Three days later *Termagant* tried again and found the gun positions abandoned. The destroyers were warned by a party of Belgian fishermen that the area was intensively mined and Keyes, who had with him the King and Queen of the Belgians, transferred to a motor boat and then to a whaler, which put the party ashore, with some difficulty, at Ostend. After a brief celebration with the jubilant town council, the party made their way back to their boat and thence to the destroyer. The King and Queen were then taken by fast CMB to the safety of Dunkirk, avoiding mines and experiencing an engine breakdown on the way.

Royalty having been successfully disposed of, it was time to set about clearing the coastal minefields, which were still, in some instances, covered by fire from a few coastal batteries which remained active. A number of paddlers and tunnel minesweepers were summoned and almost immediately the Admiralty paddler *Plumpton* struck a mine and had to be beached. This was worrying as it was high water and she was a shallow-draft vessel. Once again, the destroyers were abandoned for CMBs, which, with the tunnel sweepers, pushed cautiously on towards Zeebrugge, Keyes's own boat missing a floating horned mine 'by a wash' when travelling at thirty knots on the way. The party arrived in Zeebrugge late that evening only to find that some French motor boats had beaten them to it, and Belgian troops were in the town.

Returning to Ostend, Keyes made the mistake of setting off for Dunkirk in a dinghy with three officers and two seamen. They found a heavy swell running outside the harbour and, to their horror, as they struggled to keep the little boat head on to the waves, a searchlight came on to reveal the monitor *M21* sinking, having struck a floating mine. The dinghy returned to shore safely, although another boat sent to rescue them capsized with the loss of several men. All the following week, attempts were made to clear the shallow minefields but it was obvious that after the loss of *Plumpton*, paddlers could not be used, even at high water. Tunnel minesweepers could enter the fields, but the mines had been laid with especially tough moorings and the little sweepers could make no impression on them. Eventually, the attempt was abandoned and a specialist team of salvage men and divers had to be used to clear them. Unfortunately, *ML561* was sunk while destroying floating mines with gunfire, as a result of striking one just below the surface.

Later, when hostilities were over, it was possible to use drifters by themselves to sweep shallow fields near the Dutch and Belgian coasts where the water was very shallow and even mines sitting on the bottom were a danger. These all had to be painstakingly trawled up and exploded. There was also the dangerous job of exploding the many mines that became washed up on shore. This work was undertaken by a small flotilla of drifters based on Ostend. The crews were horrified to find that the shortage of food on the continent was much worse than at home so the problems of feeding themselves locally were dire. This was solved by designating one of the drifters as a regular fishing vessel whose duty it was to catch fish for the flotilla.

There is a story, no doubt improved in the telling, of mines being swept from the Belgian canals. This was done by using a pair of cart horses on either bank pulling a sweep between them. The mines were then blown up when the horses were well clear. The naval rating carrying out this operation found two small white ensigns to attach to the tails of the horses.

An original arrangement was devised for another detail of sweepers being used to clear the very dense minefields off the east coast of England. These were partly British protective fields and partly offensive German ones. There were so many mines of different types that sweepers found them floating all over the over the place behind their sweeps and they often drifted dangerously close to the ships themselves. No one really knew if the de-activation devices, which should have rendered them safe when detached from their moorings, were effective. A large trawl net was made up, kept open by floats and otter boards and towed behind a drifter. Inside the net was an electrically controlled mine that could be set off from on board the drifter. When the net had collected a good number of mines the tow rope was lengthened so that it was a safe distance from the drifter and the controlled mine detonated. This caused a terrific explosion as all the mines in the net went up, to the great satisfaction of all concerned.

One of the toughest clearance jobs fell to the US Navy who had to work on the vast array of mines, deep and shallow, that constituted the Northern Barrage. Most of these were antenna mines, which were especially liable to explode unexpectedly, and were liable to counter mining. There was not much experience in sweeping them. As the mines were electrically detonated, they were very dangerous to any steel vessel and, at first, a survey was made of them by a pair of wooden Lowestoft sailing fishing smacks loaned to the Americans. These were arranged to drag a sweep between them and set off into the minefield. 'It was a pretty sight', wrote an observer 'To see these little craft sailing back and forth across the minefield, wearing and tacking in unison, and keeping station with each other by furling topsails or streaming sea anchors.' A pretty sight indeed, and the smacks determined that the mines were intact and could be set off by their metal trawl wire. However, the enterprise nearly ended in disaster. Mines detonated too close to the boats, starting seams and causing severe leaks, then a heavy gale blew up and they had to struggle into shelter. By the time sweeping began in earnest, in April 1919, minesweepers had been demagnetized thus becoming much safer and non-magnetic wooden kites were supplied, but the weather was no better with bitter winds and snow storms. There were frequent instances of mines getting caught in the sweeping gear and exploding under the stern on the vessels causing damage and casualties. On one day in July, for example the sweeper *Pelican* was damaged by six mines that exploded all round her, probably as a result of counter mining. She began to sink, but *Auk* and *Eider* came alongside with pumps and were just able to keep up with the inrushing water. *Teal* then took the three ships in tow and the four sweepers struggled towards safety. Soon, a heavy westerly wind came up and the ships began to buck and plunge in the seas, breaking the pumping hoses and threatening to sink *Pelican* altogether. Most of her crew were taken off, and men were detailed to stand by with axes to cut her free as soon as she started to go down, but somehow the little ships struggled the fifty miles to Sanday Island and shelter.

By the end of September 1919 the northern barrage area was declared clear of mines. Over 21,000 mines had been swept; the remainder had either sunk, exploded spontaneously, or dragged their moorings into deeper water. It was a remarkably fine achievement by the US Navy who displayed commendable seamanship and gallantry. They were working in some of the stormiest waters in the world. Two officers and nine men were killed and twenty-three ships seriously damaged during the operation.

Sweeping up the mines in the Dardanelles was undertaken mainly by the Royal Navy and was made more difficult because no proper charts on the mines were available. The sweeping force was equipped with a number of kite balloons manned and operated by the then infant Royal Air Force. It was possible to spot mines under water in the clear water provided the weather was calm, so the balloon observer and his telephone operator could guide the sweeper to a point a few yards from the mine where a buoy would be dropped. By marking all the mines that could be seen in this way soon a pattern would become evident and the sweepers (mostly paddlers because of their shallow draft) could work up a line of mines and destroy them. This was tricky because of the strength of the current but was achieved eventually. Some of the mines, laid in very shallow water, were spotted from the air then lassoed by men standing in the bows of the sweeper. Wire nooses would then be slipped over the mine so that it could be pulled from its mooring and dealt with when it came above water. This must have been an especially ticklish operation. Over 3,000 mines were swept in the Dardanelles and adjacent waters with a loss of four sweepers and about fifty lives. Most of the casualties occurred when mines got caught up in sweeps, causing the sweeper to stop and then drift down on the current onto the next line of mines.

CHAPTER 7

Conclusion

The Russo-Japanese War had given plenty of warning that the mine was to be a key naval weapon in any future conflict. The Germans realized this, whereas the British tried, initially, to ignore it. Thanks to a courageous body of fishermen and a few determined naval officers working tirelessly in almost unbelievably difficult conditions, the mine menace was eventually contained but never eliminated.

The British were ultimately able to use their own mines to make a major contribution to the vital anti U-boat struggle and to the policy of blockading Germany, which eventually led to the collapse of German morale and the end of the war. It is no exaggeration to say that the anti-submarine mines that were used in such profusion in 1917/18, together with the convoy system, saved Britain from being starved out of the war by the U-boat campaign against merchant shipping. Although the total number of U-boats sunk was small in comparison to those destroyed by other methods, the minefields made their operations so difficult that their effectiveness was greatly diminished. The intensive mining of the eastern North Sea also contributed to Germany's eventual collapse. By pinning the High Seas Fleet in its bases, to such an extent that it could not even undertake exercises safely, the British offensive mining campaign contributed to the collapse of fleet discipline and hence to the popular revolt against the Kaiser's government, which resulted in the Armistice.

The transformation of British naval thinking had been dramatic. Talk of 'the battle fleet' and of 'a second Trafalgar' had become strangely obsolete. This war was won by small ships and submarines operating in enemy waters, and by minesweepers doggedly keeping channels clear. It was perhaps a disappointing lesson for the Royal Navy to learn, but by 1918 it had been well learnt and applied with vigour, resourcefulness and skill. The role of the great battleships was simply to remain a 'fleet in being'– a deterrent held in harbour, not an active fleet blockading off enemy coasts like Nelson's navy.

Mines have continued to evolve since 1918. During the Second World War, mines dropped from aircraft and laid by ships formed an important part of British and German strategy. Magnetic and acoustic mines, as well as conventional contact mines, were used by both sides, and increasingly sophisticated systems were used for mine clearance. Since 1945 the unimaginable power of nuclear explosives has been applied to mine design. Correspondingly, mine hunting remains one of the most critical sectors of naval warfare. Mines are still a weapon that can be effectively employed by a weak naval power (or, perhaps, a terrorist) against a strong one. Astonishingly, they have proved at the same time to be the one naval armament that retains its deadly effectiveness almost indefinitely and is extremely cheap to procure and deploy. North Korea used primitive contact mines in the Korean War, causing both Britain and the US to build entirely new classes

of minesweeper, now called Mine Counter Measures Vessels
(MCVs). The Vietnam War saw the deployment by North
Vietnam of Russian mines made before the First World War.
The result was described by Rear Admiral A. Smith USN, the
Commander of Amphibious Forces, in the following terms:

> We lost control of the seas to a nation without a navy using
> pre World War One weapons, laid by vessels that were in
> use at the time of Christ.

In the Iran/Iraq War and the First Gulf War, mines, some of
them of the same vintage and from the same Russian source,
were deployed by both Iran and Iraq. Serious mine damage
was inflicted on three major American warships, USS *Tripoli*,
Princeton and *Samuel B Roberts*. Apart from hampering
operations and requiring the dispatch of a force of MCVs
from the UK and elsewhere, the damage to these three ships
cost many millions of dollars to repair. The mines involved
cost the Iraqis $30,000. They were put in position by an
ancient Japanese landing craft, probably assisted by small
motor fishing dhows. One is forcefully reminded of the
Dardanelles campaign of 1915.

Index

Abdiel Minelayer 78, 79, 94, 120,
  135, 145, 146
Acoustic Devices 125, 129, 135,
  160
Adkins Lieut. RN 70
Albatross Minelayer 51
American Civil War 16 et seq
American War of Independence
  9 et seq
Amphion HMS 47, 51
Antenna Mines 141, 142, 144,
  155
Audacious HMS 1 et seq 61

B.11 101
Bacon Admiral Sir Reginald 89,
  127, 128
Beatty Admiral Sir David 125,
  127
Bell Lieutenant RN 58, 59
Beresford Admiral Sir Charles
  29, 127
Berlin Liner 5 et seq
Bremmer & Bremse Minelayers
  94
Bushnell David 10

Carden Admiral Sir Sackville
  101 et seq
Charlton Admiral Ned 34 et seq

Churchill Winston 74, 102, 105,
  114
Conan Doyle Trawler 32
Cottingham Freighter 64
Crimean War 15
Crossley Lieutenant RNR 54

Dorothy Grey Trawler 31, 32
Dover Barrage 128
Drifting Mines 12

E.11 108
E Class 108, 119, 120, 122
Egg Mine 125
Elia Mine 125

Fielding Martin 38 et seq
Fisher Admiral Jacky 34, 102,
  113, 127
Folkestone Griz Nez Barrage
  116, 130, 131, 133
Fulton David 11 et seq
Furbringer Capt. Werner 89, 136

Geehl Lt Col 100, 106
Goeben 97 109
Goodenough Commodore
  "Barge" 2
Ground Mines 12

H.II Mine 123, 141, 145, 147
Hague Convention 45
Harwood John 36 et seq
Hertz Horn 17 et seq 25, 26, 46,
    101, 106, 114, 118, 120, 123

International Mine Clearance
    Committee 149
Irresistible HMS 106

Jellicoe Admiral Sir John 2 et
    seq 34, 70, 71, 73, 74, 76, 120,
    124, 127, 132
Jutland Battle of 74, 76 et seq

Keyes Admiral Sir Roger 47, 48,
    56, 99, 106, 107, 108, 127 et seq
    152, 153
King Edward VII Battleship 71
Kitchener General 76
Kolberg Minelayer 52, 53
Konigin Louise Minelayer 46, 47

Leon mines 13, 14, 79, 100, 145
Limpet mines 8, 15
Liverpool HMS 1 et seq
Losses due to Mines 148

Maas Minefield 81, 93
Magnetic Mines 125, 129, 147
Makaroff Admiral 19
Manchester Commerce Freighter
    7, 35
Meteor Minelayer 69, 70
Minnesota USS Battleship 92
Moewe Minelayer 71
Monitors 81, 89, 121, 132, 152,
    153
Moored mines 14

Nasmith Martin Lieutenant RN
    108
Nautilus Minelayer 51

Naval Spherical Mine 16, 27, 76,
    112, 118, 123
New York USS Battleship 81
Nobel Mines 15
Northern Barrage 139, 142, 144,
    145, 150, 155, 156

Ocean HMS 106
Olympic Liner 7
Ommanney Admiral Sir Robert
    113, 114
Ostfriesland Battleship 79
Ottley Lieut. RN 23

Paddle Sweepers 39 et seq 57 et
    seq 71, 72, 84 et seq 95, 134,
    153, 157
Para vane 72, 73, 82, 83, 99, 107
Parsons Godfrey Lieutenant RN
    53
Parsons Lieut RN 118 et seq
Plummet System 23, 24, 26, 123,
    124
Preston Lionel Commander 29,
    53, 54, 124, 150
Princess Margaret Minelayer
    117, 121, 145, 146

Q Message 35
Queen Elizabeth Battleship 102,
    105

Robeck Admiral 105, 106
Room 40, 70, 123
Russo Japanese War 18 et seq

S119 Destroyer 51
San Diego USS Cruiser 92
Scheer Admiral 73, 74, 120
Schleswig-Holstein War 15
Seydlitz Battle cruiser 75, 76
Sloop 56, 71, 72, 74, 81, 90

Thompson Lieut. RN 84
Tunnel Minesweepers 61, 87, 153

U.C. Class 64, 65, 88, 89, 128, 129
U.117 90 et seq
U.156 92
U.75 76
U.B. Class 68
U.C. 44, 88, 128
U.E. Class 65, 67, 90
UC.30 122
UC.75 122

Vernon HMS 23, 25, 112, 148
Von Knorr Capt 70

War Channel 53, 57, 59, 81
Warrander Admiral Sir George 1 et seq
Weymss Admiral 132

Yorck Cruiser 52

Zeebrugge 47, 48, 50, 68, 81, 114, 117, 121, 135, 146, 151, 153